WILD DUCKS
FLYING BACKWARD

WILD DUCKS
FLYING BACKWARD

the short writings of
TOM ROBBINS

NO EXIT PRESS

This edition published in 2006 by No Exit Press
P.O.Box 394, Harpenden, Herts, AL5 1XJ
www.noexit.co.uk

Reprinted 2006, 2007, 2013, 2015, 2016

A CIP catalogue record for this book is available from the British Library.

ISBN 13: 978-1-84243-171-9

6 8 10 9 7

Typeset by Avocet Typeset, Chilton, Aylesbury, Bucks
Printed in Great Britain by Clays Ltd, St Ives plc

For David Hirshey, who let me run with the bulls, and for Miss Indiana Cheerleader and the Bat Girl of Bleecker Street, who threw petals at me along the way.

Author's Note

The reader who might notice slight discrepancies between some of the pieces in *Wild Ducks Flying Backward* and the way they appeared in those venues where they were initially published may be assured that there's a simple explanation. Some of the original articles had been pruned and truncated, usually for reasons of space, and I've restored those cuts. In addition, while reviewing the older pieces, I found that I had occasionally used words or phrases for which I now saw more interesting, effective alternatives. What could I do but substitute? A writer who passes up any opportunity to refresh his language is not a writer you can expect to meet in Heaven.

T. R.

Your true guide drinks from an undammed stream.
                                    —Rumi
Never enter a house that does not have furniture music.
                                    —Erik Satie

Contents

CONTENTS

CONTENTS

RESPONSES

WILD DUCKS
FLYING BACKWARD

Introduction

It's six o'clock in the afternoon, approximately, give or take a tick or two, and the sun's attention span is rapidly shrinking. The sun, we might say, should we choose to venture further down the path of anthropomorphic hyperbole, has seen quite enough of you for one day and is entertaining other options. Weary of the old ice-cream castle Judy Collins routine, clouds, too, are shifting priorities, gathering forces, adopting attitudes. By nightfall, you could be in for some rain. Perhaps freezing rain. Even snow. Obviously, we're privy neither to your whereabouts nor your season. You're in freaking North Dakota for all we know. November.

What we do know is that you have availed yourself of the most recent book by novelist Tom Robbins, and what we can *assume,* though it may be only a conceit, is that you have every intention of beginning it this evening (you couldn't very well have begun it at work today), so if external weather conditions prove foul, so much the better. Should it pelt, should it blow, the cozy factor (almost always a boon to literary experience) will increase several-fold, thereby fertilizing the narcotic poppy of reading pleasure.

The climate indoors is another matter. Serious reading is hardly a social activity and every halfway serious reader is perpetually subject to a form of coitus interruptus. Family members or friends who lack the desire, the courage, or the opportunity to burst in on you when there's some indication that you could be sexually entwined will seldom hesitate to interject themselves between you and a page, even though the act of reading is often as intimate and intense as a full-fledged carnal embrace. You must take steps to ensure your privacy.

It's a Monday, so more than likely your male companion and his buddy, eager for three solid hours of beer commercials and televised football, have already commandeered the sofa. Good. That frees up the bedroom.

Or, switching genders (though not necessarily), your girl-friend's in bed with monthly cramps, a heating pad on that sweet little tummy you so love to nuzzle, medication making her sleepy, soft rock on the radio. You suppress a smile of relief. The sofa is all yours.

Of course, if you live alone, both bed and sofa are available – you have only to choose your spot, change into something comfortable, adjust the lighting, and disconnect the phone.

No, there's one other thing: this is a Tom Robbins tome you're about to sit down with, and while special fortification is certainly not mandatory, it wouldn't hurt to adjust your mental thermostat a bit. Nothing drastic. No overhaul. You know. Just rotate your tires. Yet, while a weak gin-and-tonic might go well with, say, E. M. Forster or Virginia Woolf, while a tumbler of bourbon might help you wash Faulkner down, Robbins requires a more – shall we say, *exotic*? – accompaniment.

Stealthily, nonchalantly, you make your way to your dresser, open your underwear drawer, dig out that bottle of anaïs nin (green label) you've been hoarding there. Careful! Don't pour too much. Remember what happened that time on your birthday. Besides, ever since the revolution in Punto del Visionario the stuff has been almost impossible to find. And by the way, in case you haven't heard, it's been placed on the gov-ernment's list of controlled substances.

Okay. At last you're set. You prop up your feet (we should always read with our feet up, even on the subway or a bus), and retrieve the book, feeling in your hands the weight, the newness, the *bookness* of it. For a brief second you close your eyes, sip your libation (Jesus! Wow! No wonder there're two dots over the *ï*!), and allow yourself to wonder what Robbins is up to this time around. What strange lights on what distant mountainside have attracted his focus? Over whose campfire – gypsy? guerrilla? Girl Scout? shaman? – has he been toasting his ideas, his images, his figures of speech?

Curiosity suitably aroused, anticipation at a delicious pitch, you take in a small breath and open the book and . . . Whoa! Wait a damn minute. Hold on. This isn't the new Tom Robbins novel. Oh, it's by Robbins all right, but . . . You look again at the cover. *The Short Writings of* . . . It's printed right there on the jacket. Maybe it could have been in bigger type but it isn't as if you've been tricked. It's your own fault, you should have paid closer attention. This will teach you to dash into a bookshop on your lunch hour. *Wild Ducks Flying Backward* is not a novel at all.

Somewhat disgruntled, you riffle the pages. Hmm? Travel articles. Riffs on various exceptional people. A short story or two. Poems. (Robbins, at any rate, calls them "poems": your old English professor would probably shake his head and call them something else entirely.) Essays. Responses. Musings. A treatment for a movie you'd wager will never be made.

There are even a couple of examples of the author's art criticism, included, you suppose, to demonstrate to those who might suspect otherwise that a man's expressed preference for right-brain activity need not necessarily constitute an admission of weakness on the left. In fact, so sober and coolly cerebral is Robbins's analysis of the painter Morris Louis that you find it difficult to believe it could have been written in the same year (1967) and by the same person (Robbins) as the overheated, rocked-out, purple-lipped paean to The Doors also contained herein. The contrast both intrigues and confounds you.

About the same time that young Tom was deconstructing modern art and eulogizing psychedelic rockers, he was deciding once and for all to move his professional residence to the land of make-believe, the land of effects as opposed to facts, the country where Style is king and Paradox and Enigma (which must hide between the lines in reportage) are granted diplomatic immunity. He began writing his first novel in 1968 and he's made it clear that if he's remembered, he wants it to be for his fiction. Still, for whatever reason – to meet an editor's challenge, maybe, or to charm the groceries – the novelist has over the years made occasional forays across the inky divide into journalism. Considering the source, aren't you at least tempted to test the results? And what about that short story, the one he calls "Moonlight Whoopee Cushion Sonata"?

You're warm, snug, alone, loosely clothed, and the anaïs nin (green label) is working your blood like a Vegas entertainer working a room. If you don't burrow further into this modest if unusual collection, what else can you possibly do with yourself tonight?

You don't have to answer that.

TRAVEL
ARTICLES

Canyon of the Vaginas

When one is on a pilgrimage to the Canyon of the Vaginas, one has to be careful about asking directions.

I mean, there're some pretty rough ol' dudes in west-central Nevada. One knows the ol' dudes are rough when one observes that they eat with their hats on.

Nine days I was in the high desert between Winnemucca and Las Vegas, during which time I never witnessed a male homo sapiens take his noontide nor his evening repast with an exposed bean. In every instance, a grimy bill or brim shaded the fellow's victuals from the vulgar eye of light. I assumed that they breakfasted *en chapeau* as well, but by the hour that your pilgrim sat down to *his* flapjacks, the rough ol' dudes had already gone off to try to strike it rich.

When a man's brain is constantly heated by thoughts of striking it rich, thoughts that don't fade much at mealtime, perhaps he requires some sort of perpetual head cover to cool the cerebral machinery. On the other hand, since they live in relatively close proximity to America's major nuclear test site, a nerve-gas depot, several mysterious airfields, and numerous depositories for our government's nasty toxic secrets, maybe the rough ol' dudes are just trying to prevent their haircuts from ever flickering in the dark. If I lived in west-central Nevada, I might dine in gloves and a Mylex suit.

Naturally, one has to wonder if the men of Nevada also sleep in their hats. More pointedly, do they sleep with their wives, girlfriends, and thoroughly legal prostitutes in their hats? I intended to interview a Nevada woman or two on the subject, but never quite got around to it. However, something at the Canyon of the Vaginas gave me reason to believe that the answer is affirmative. Of that, more later.

Getting back on course, beneath those baseball caps that advertise brands of beer or heavy equipment, under those genuine imitation Stetsons, there're some rough ol' hangovers being processed and some rough ol' ideas being entertained. One simply does not approach a miner, a wrangler, a prospector, a gambler, a Stealth pilot, a construction sweat hog, or sandblasted freebooter and interrupt his thoughts about big, fast bucks and those forces – environmental legislation, social change, loaded dice, et cetera – that could stand between him and big, fast bucks; one simply does not march up to such a man, a man who lifts his crusty lid to no one, and ask:

"Sir, might you possibly direct me to the Canyon of the Vaginas?"

* * * * * * * * * * *

Should readers desire to make their own pilgrimage to the Canyon of the Vaginas – and it is, after all, one of the few holy places left in America – they'll have to find it by themselves. Were one to inquire of its whereabouts at a bar or gas station (in west-central Nevada they're often one and the same, complete with slot machines), the best that one could hope for is that a dude would wink and aim one at the pink gates of Bobbie's Cottontail Ranch, or whatever the nearest brothel might be called.

In the improbable event that he fails to misinterpret one's

inquiry, and/or to take sore offense at it, a dude still isn't likely
to further one's cause. For that matter, save for the odd archeologist, neither is anybody else. The population of Nevada
arises every morning, straightens its hat, swallows a few
aspirin, and trucks off to try to strike it rich without so much
as a nervous suspicion that the Canyon of the Vaginas lies
within its domain.

Your pilgrim learned of it from a Salt Lake City artist who
has hiked and camped extensively in the high deserts of the
Great Basin. The man drew me a fairly specific map, but I, in
good conscience, cannot pass along the details. My reluctance
to share is rooted neither in selfishness nor elitism, but in the
conviction that certain aspects of the canyon are quite fragile
and in need of protection.

Not that genuflecting hordes are likely to descend upon it:
the canyon is remote; troubled, according to season, by killer
sun, ripping wind, and blinding blizzard; and is reached by a
road that nobody making monthly car payments should even
think of driving. Still, there are plenty of new-agers with the
leisure and energy to track down yet another "power center,"
and plenty of curiosity seekers with an appetite for the exotic
souvenir. Surely I'll be forgiven if I'm ever so slightly discreet.

Besides, what kind of pilgrimage would it be if it didn't
contain some element of hardship and enigma? The quest is
essential to the ritual. To orient ourselves at the interface of
the visible and invisible worlds – which may be the purpose of
all pilgrimages – we must embrace the search as well as its
goal. If our journey into the heart (or vagina) of meaning
resembles in any appreciable manner our last trip to the shopping mall, we're probably doing something wrong.

I can disclose this much: to arrive at the Canyon of the
Vaginas, your pilgrim had to travel a ways on Highway 50, a
blue guitar string of asphalt accurately described by postcards
and brochures as the Most Lonesome Road in America. It will

impress some readers as poignantly correct that so many vaginas are reached only by a route of almost legendary loneliness. Others won't have that reaction at all.

* * * * * * * * * * *

Physically, my pilgrimage commenced in downtown Seattle. Downtown Seattle has long been my "stomping grounds," as they say, although in the past couple of years it's lost its homey air. A side effect of Reaganomics was skyscraper fever. Developers, taking advantage of lucrative tax breaks, voodoo-pinned our city centers with largely unneeded office towers. In downtown Seattle, for some reason, most of the excess buildings are beige. Seattleites complain of beige à vu: the sensation that they've seen that color before.

In any case, it was in a Seattle parking lot, flanked by beige edifices, that I exchanged cars with my chiropractor. He took my customized Camaro Z-28 convertible, a quick machine whose splendid virtues do not include comfort on long-distance hauls; I took his big, new Mercedes.

If, indeed, the reader should decide to motor to Nevada and it proves to exceed an afternoon's jaunt, may I suggest swapping cars with a chiropractor? Chiropractors' cars are not like yours or mine. Theirs tend to be massage parlors on wheels, equipped with the latest breakthroughs in therapeutic seating, lumbar cushions, and vertebrae-aligning headrests. It's like rolling along in a technological spa. The driver can get a spinal adjustment and a speeding ticket simultaneously.

So relaxed was I in that tea-green Mercedes that I didn't look around when I heard my chiropractor burn a quarter inch of rubber off the Camaro's tires. In a certain way, it was reminiscent of the movie *Trading Places*. As the good doctor tore off to drag sorority row at the University of Washington, I oozed through the beige maze with a serene, chiropractic smile, braking tenderly in front of Alexa's apartment, and then in front of Jon's.

For days to come, the three of us, Alexa, Jon, and your pilgrim, would take turns piloting the doctor's clinical dreamboat along tilting tables of rural landscape. Once we'd crossed the tamed Columbia and were traversing the vastness of eastern Oregon, once we were out of the wet zone and into the dry zone, out of the vegetable zone and into the meat zone, out of the fiberglass-shower-stall zone and into the metal-shower-stall zone, we would glide through a seemingly endless variety of ecosystems, most of them virtually relieved of the more obvious signs of human folly, all of them unavoidably gorgeous.

Some of the hills were shaped like pyramids, others resembled the contents of Brunhilde's bodice. One was so vibrantly purple-black that we suspected we'd discovered the mother lode where eye shadow was mined. There were craters and slumps, stacks and slides, alkali lakes and sand dunes, gorges and passes, fossil beds, dust devils, and enormous ragged buttes that could have been cruise ships for honeymooning trolls. We followed chatty little creeks, spilling their creek guts to anybody who'd listen; we swerved to miss antelope, reduced dead jackrabbits to two dimensions, honked at happy dogs and range steers, photographed gap-toothed windmills and churches in which no collection plate would ever circulate again, inhaled sage until our sinuses gobbled, and cast self-righteous judgment on the bored adolescent gunmen and beered-up Cattle Xing terrorists who'd blown a Milky Way of holes into each and every road sign.

It delighted me that the Canyon of the Vaginas was out here smack dab in the middle of the Wild American West. How swell that in the Old West of gunfights and land grabs, massacres and gold rushes, bushwhackings and horsewhippings, missions, saloons, boot hills, and forts, there existed a culture that celebrated with artistic eloquence and spiritual fervor the most intimate feature of the feminine anatomy.

Imagine Custer's cavalry troop thundering innocently over a ridge, only to come face-to-face with (gasp!) the pink, the moist, the yielding, the delicately curly. Imagine a Saturday matinee: *Roy Rogers at the Canyon of the Vaginas.*

Mentally, emotionally, my pilgrimage began back in my late twenties or early thirties, whenever it was that it first occurred to me that the female genitals were literally divine. In the Orient, especially in the religious systems of Tibet and India, that notion has prevailed since dimmest antiquity, and as a matter of fact, there are yonic symbols in the caves of Paleolithic Europe (dating back twenty thousand years) that are indistinguishable from those venerated today by the tantric cults of the Himalayas.

When I read how, among the practitioners of tantra, the vulva is adored as the organ for the generation of world and time, it struck a resonant chord. From that day on, I have been seeking the American tantra, which is to say, I've been seeking American images that promote that inner intensity of feminine sexuality, whose source is the Goddess of Creation.

Among the examples that have caught my attention are the bubblegum-colored underpants that Bonnie Parker left behind to taunt the cops when she and Clyde Barrow flew the coop. I was convinced, you see, that the American tantra must be as different from the Asian tantra as we Americans – sweet gangsters at heart – are different from pious Asians. In the modern sense, I still think that's true, but until I learned of the Canyon of the Vaginas, I'd neglected to consider the tantric contribution of American Indians.

Having meditated on and received inspiration from such ostensibly profane icons as Bonnie's panties (she purchased them, by the way, at a small-town Kansas dime store in 1934), it fazed me only a smidgen to discover that what may be the ultimate tantric tribute on our continent is located in west-central Nevada. Even that trace of skepticism vanished when I remembered that the Goddess of Creation also serves as the Goddess of Destruction.

* * * * * * * * * * *

If something is so hazardous and destructive and ugly and spooky that we don't know what to do with it, we stick it in Nevada. The state is blotched with "Danger Areas," immense, guarded, off limits, concealing every imaginable kind of high-tech poison, as well as the various weapons systems that sup on or excrete those poisons. In Nevada, a fluffy little cloud can suddenly exterminate a whole flock of sheep. And Nevada is the place the Bomb calls home.

Even the brothels, sanctioned by the state because it's believed that military men, cowboys, and miners can't function efficiently without the help of whores, even the brothels are a sort of dumping ground. As for casinos, they could be viewed as dumping grounds for money; at least, that's been your pilgrim's experience.

We dump on Nevada because Nevada seems so useless and empty, because it seems that there is less there there than the there that Gertrude Stein couldn't find in Oakland. That, of course, is an illusion. Any couch turnip who's caught *The Wonderful World of Disney* knows that the desert is teeming.

There aren't a lot of *humans* in Nevada, relatively speaking, but considering the lifestyles of those who are there, considering that the thickest crowds are in the barrooms and that the barrooms are open around the clock (prevailing custom among the rough ol' dudes is that if you strike it rich, you get drunk to celebrate, and if you don't, you get drunk to forget), considering that the chief complaint in those barrooms is, "They didn't let us win in Vietnam," considering that the average Nevadan resides in a mobile double-wide with nothing in its grassless yard except a satellite dish as big as a moon, considering that the majority is poised to get the hell out the instant it strikes it rich, and, finally, considering that the rock group Men Without Hats is permanently barred from the Nevada Top Forty, it's doubtlessly a blessing that there aren't more citizens around to further mug the countryside and zap its small creatures.

The trouble with Nevada is that it thinks it's Alaska. It thinks it's the last frontier, at a time when the last frontier has moved beyond Anchorage to the other side of Jupiter. Regardless, Nevada is permeated by the frontier mentality, with its love of guns and booze and its hankering for bonanza. Much of it is nutty and most of it is crude (the Nevada state song is the exaggerated belch), yet Alexa, Jon, and I were quick to agree that even these ersatz Kit Carsonisms radiated authenticity when compared to the gentrification that is sugaring the bowels of urban America.

For example, it was strangely refreshing to read in the *Tonopah Times-Bonanza and Goldfield News* of not one but two recent ax murders. In our more chic towns and cities, killers no longer address victims with axes. They use sushi knives on them. Or shove baby bok choy up their noses.

Actually, before my pilgrimage was over, I wouldn't have minded a leaf or two of bok choy. Aside from the iceberg lettuce mailed in from California, there's not a fresh vegetable in all of west-central Nevada. The state bird of Nevada is the chicken-fried steak – and the labored flapping of its gravy-slathered wings (admittedly delicious) only fans the flames of frontierism. An organism running on brussels sprouts probably isn't as inclined to shoot up road signs or to share its habitat with bombing ranges and plutonium dumps as one that's running on hammered beef.

At any rate, the Goddess of Destruction dances on in

Nevada, fangs dribbling steak juice, the desert sun aglint on her necklace of skulls. In tantra, she is loved not one smooch less than her benevolent twin. Your pilgrim is slowly learning to love the Dark Dancer as well. Yes, but it was her flip side, the Good Witch, that enticed him to Nevada, where natural beauty struggles to hold its own against the treacherous ticky-tack spawned by the greed and fear of men. Surely, at the Canyon of the Vaginas, the Mother of Creation would prevail.

Alas, on that May afternoon when finally we neared the canyon, Ms. Destruction appeared to be directing the show. The wind was gusting at 70 miles an hour, and with every windshieldful of sand and snow, the chiropractic Mercedes whined as if its back hurt. Visibility was so poor that we asked Alexa to drive. At twenty-five, she was far less experienced behind the wheel than Jon or I, but she happens to be, first, female, and second, a gifted psychic. We reasoned that it would take more than a spring storm to prevent those sacred yonis from showing up on her radar.

She rewarded our trust by turning off the main highway and onto an even more lonesome road, a one-lane, unpaved car path that stretched across the sagebrush flats like a chalk line on the tennis court of the buffalo. For nineteen miles we followed this lane, seemingly into the Void. As pebbles pinged against its underbelly and juniper twigs clawed at its precious Prussian paint, the Mercedes sobbed for autobahns, crying out, *"Die Stadt! Wo ist die Stadt?"* One might say that we were in the middle of nowhere, especially if one were the type who believes midtown Manhattan to be the center of everywhere.

Through rents in the curtain of snowy dust, we could see that we were entering the foothills of a low mountain range. "According to the map, we're only a pubic hair away," said I, and moments later, Alexa stopped the car. Well, if there was holy real estate in the vicinity, it wasn't exactly advertised.

Nothing caught our vision beyond the boundlessness of space. The silence was so deep that even the gale seemed to be wearing moccasins. And when we opened the doors, a great essence of sage rushed in. It smelled as if every grandmother in the U.S.A. was simultaneously stuffing a turkey.

We stumbled about pessimistically in that Thanks-givingscape for a while. And abruptly, there it was! There was no mistaking it. We couldn't make out details, but the site was so charged it practically had an aura around it. The three of us glanced at one another knowingly, then, bucking the wind, took off at a fast trot. And we didn't slow down until we were surrounded by a plenitude of pudenda.

I looked one of the specimens right in the eye. "Doctor Vagina, I presume?"

* * * * * * * * * * *

The official name of the place is innocuous: North Canyon. It's quite narrow and fewer than two hundred yards long. The entire canyon is rather vaginal in shape, terminating in a scooped-out basin of white alkali that those so inclined could read as *uterus* or *womb*. The canyon floor is hirsute with juniper and sage.

According to Jon's compass, North Canyon lies on a perfect east–west axis. The entrance is at the east end, where it's most narrow. Obviously, there's a strong solar connection. When the sun rises each morning, it passes through the natural gateway, moving up the passage to the "womb." The volcanic-ash-flow walls are a yellowish orangish reddish tan, which is to say, the palette of the sun.

Both facing walls of the canyon entrance are covered with petroglyphs. No, somehow "covered" doesn't do them justice. They are *singing* with petroglyphs.

A petroglyph is a drawing that has been pecked, incised, or

scratched into stone. Frequently, as is the case at North Canyon, the rock exposed by the pecking is appreciably lighter in color than the outer surfaces, which have been patinated by millennia of oxidation. This affords the design excellent contrast, although as the centuries hop along, the uncovered rock, too, gradually darkens.

There are innumerable examples of petroglyphs in the western U.S., some of them ceremonial in intention, some mnemonic, some totemic (clan symbols), and some, it would appear, just an outburst of pleasurable doodling. The majority of the drawings are concerned with game, for the artists who chipped them were hunter-gatherers, and they may or may not include human figures. In addition, there are highly mannered petroglyphs and examples that are completely abstract.

The rock panels at the portal to North Canyon support a smattering of curvilinear abstractions, including the mysterious dot patterns that are characteristic of Great Basin rock art. There are a goodly number of enlarged bird tracks, apparently the symbol of the Bird Clan. And there is a rendering of a European-style house and a miner's charcoal kiln, proving that Indians were still pecking at the site well into the nineteenth century. By far the dominant motif of North Canyon, however, is the stylized vagina.

The vagina glyph is not exactly rare on the rocks of the West, but at no other site is it found in such concentration or profusion. In an old shaman's cave on nearby Hickison Summit, there's a lone yoni of great loveliness, but North Canyon, oh mama! North Canyon is a *festival* of female genitalia, a labial showcase, a vulval jubilee, and clearly the wellspring of our indigenous tantra.

Rome wasn't built in a day, to coin a phrase, and neither was this vaginal display. Worn, overlapped, and overlaid, the drawings were pecked over a long period of time. Human habitation in the region dates back ten thousand years.

Volcanic ash is too soft to hold an image for such a lengthy period, but one of the few archeologists to give North Canyon more than a passing nod has estimated that it could maintain a vulva in fairly good condition for about five centuries. Shelley Winters, eat your heart out.

Although the Paiute may have had a finger in them, the best guess is that North Canyon's murals are the work of the Shoshoni, a seminomadic civilization of underestimated complexity. The question is, Why? Why did they adorn the sun gate of Nevada's high desert with scores of mannered pudenda? Perhaps North Canyon was a fertility motel that Shoshoni couples checked into in order to ensure conception. Perhaps it involved a type of coming-of-age ritual. Perhaps – and your pilgrim favors this theory – it was intended as an homage to that feminine principle that the Shoshoni recognized to be the genesis of continuous creation: Earth herself; mother of deer, mother of trout, mother of grass seeds, bulbs, and roots, mother of the ground on which they walked and the cliffs that sheltered them. Maybe, on the other hand, North Canyon was purely sexual, a horny pecking of individual lust into the enduring dimension of stone.

It's reported that there are heterosexual males who can stare down a vulva, real or rendered, and register not an erg of prurience, but, honestly now, do you trust these guys? Would you want your daughter to marry one?

At any rate, many of North Canyon's vaginas are bull's-eyed with holes that have been "worried" by sticks. Assuming that the sticks were surrogate penises, there definitely was some sort of copulative magic going on. The energy of the place is openly erotic, and at the same time keenly spiritual. Presumably, the Shoshoni would have found no contradiction.

We stood there in a whirl of white flakes, eating a full ration of grit, letting the wind paint our ligaments blue, feeling somewhat sexy and somewhat religious, feeling a little like laughing and a little like weeping, until we got so cold we could no longer feel anything but the necessity of a steaming bath. Since the nearest public lodging was more than a hundred miles away, we set out for it at once, saving a closer examination of the curious canyon for a more hospitable day.

* * * * * * * * * * *

That evening, in the dining room of Tonopah's Mizpah Hotel, the chicken-fried steak was delivered to Alexa, a vegetarian, while Jon, a raging carnivore, received the bowl of iceberg lettuce. The aging waitress grinned at the mistake, and tugged at the lapels of her dotted-swiss uniform. "Does the right table count for anything?" she asked. Apparently not, for the hot turkey sandwich that your pilgrim ordered (all that sagebrush had awakened a most nostalgic craving) landed on a table across the room, where it was instantly devoured by a man wearing a hat.

While our waitress labored to correct the mix-up, the lights went off. Then, on again. Off. On. Off. On. At least four times. "Happens all the time," said the waitress. "Not to worry. It's just the wind knocking two wires together."

Jon found the explanation less than plausible, but as I suffered the long wait for a turkey sandwich to call my own, it occurred to me that here was a pretty good metaphor for west-central Nevada: two wires knocking together in the wind. In the high desert, the present knocks against the past, development knocks against nature, repression against indulgence, reality against dream, masculine against feminine, the Goddess of Destruction against the Goddess of Creation, the Atomic Proving Grounds against the Canyon of the Vaginas.

For two blustery days, we holed up in the hotel, chasing fruit around the cylinder of a slot machine and watching garbage-can lids UFO past the leaded windows. On the third day, the wind fell over dead and the temperature rose forty degrees. When we drove back to North Canyon, the sky was as blue as our waitress's beehive, and a silky calm lay upon the land. Inside the canyon, the peace index tripled. It struck us as a haven, a refuge, a place where even the undeserving might be safe. Small and sweet, the canyon was nonetheless so powerful that its vectors held one's soul upright, afloat, as if in metaphysical brine.

Obviously, the Shoshoni hadn't settled on this spot arbitrarily. On a practical level, it offered protection and water, for its cliffs are high and there's a spring at the "uterus" end. Then, there's the matter of its solar alignment. These facts fail to explain its magic, however, an intrinsic presence that was merely enhanced by the hanging of vaginal wallpaper.

Incapable of solving the greater mystery, we were content to sit, stroll, and loll in private communion with the disembodied organs that surrounded us there. I could almost smell the sea in them, feel their merry, saline humidity against my cheek. Like a dolphin, a vagina wears a perpetual smile, a grin as sloppy and loving as the cradle we all rocked out of. Even in the desert, such bogs do not dry up but glisten invitingly enough to make one suspect that little warm marshes dominate the topography of Paradise.

Later in the day, exploring the canyon's middle section, we came upon what might have been Paradise Swamp itself. There on the southern wall (it seemed impossible that we'd missed it earlier) was the queen of the yonis. It was eighteen feet tall (the other vulval images seldom topped ten inches), circular, with a dark vertical gash and a broadcast wattage that could've carried its salty song to the moon. Truly the grandma, the great-grandma of vaginas, it had been embellished by pecking tools, but apparently was a natural formation.

We debated whether this geological yoni might not have been the inspiration for the petroglyphs. It carried life in it –

that life that is self-renewing and outside history – the way a bomb carries death. This goddess-size orifice might have filled the Shoshoni with wonder, binding them to the flesh that was their origin and to the earth in which their journey ultimately would end.

Jon with his camera and sketch pads, Alexa with her tarot cards, and your pilgrim with his catalog of quirks, each of us would leave North Canyon with the profound impression that contemporary society lacks any equivalent of it, and that we're the poorer for that. We sensed, moreover, that in our remove from nature and those forces that our ancestors knew intimately yet seldom named, we've lost something so important that its loss is akin to literal amputation. Without a Canyon of the Vaginas in which to peck our American tantra, in which to connect our hormones to the stars, we may be becoming psychological paraplegics.

* * * * * * * * * * *

Toward the close of day, we strolled up to the western end of the canyon to observe, as the Shoshoni certainly did before us, the setting sun. Mountain bluebirds were caroling from the juniper bushes, lizards were using their tails to write love letters in the sand, and I was meditating on Lawrence of Arabia's remark that he adored the desert because it was so clean, when I stepped in a pile of regrettably fresh antelope dung. While scraping my shoe, I glanced up an incline and spotted a suspiciously marked boulder sitting off to one side.

Upon inspection, the rock proved to have been graced with what may have been the oldest vaginal glyph at the site. It was both more eroded and more naturalistic than the stylized clusters at the entrance. That, however, wasn't what caught my eye. It turned out that this rock, and it alone, had been pecked upon by white men.

There were a couple of English words cut in the stone. They were less than legible, but from their dark color and serif lettering, we could tell that they'd been inscribed by settlers, perhaps at the turn of the century. There was also a figure on the boulder. A caucasian figure. A male figure. And how.

The honky dude sported a massive, saw-log erection (doesn't phallic graffiti invariably distort in the direction of largeness?), and it was pointed at the vagina like a cannon at a clam. The clumsiness of the execution, the image's total lack of emotional subtlety or spiritual dimension underscores the difference between so-called primitive cultures and those of the European invaders. It's the difference between harmony and aggression, wisdom and shallowness, art and pornography.

Although safely out of the state now, I still wouldn't want to say that the figure is indicative of a "dick first" attitude that continues to epitomize west-central Nevada. Nevertheless, I should mention one further thing about the man carved on the rock. As he moves to possess the object of his sexual passion, the rough ol' dude is wearing a hat.

Esquire, 1988

Two in the Bush

So you tell your girlfriend you're going to take her on a holiday to one of the most romantic spots on earth, and after she has tastefully demonstrated her gratitude and delight, she asks how she should pack. For the mountains? For the shore? For the samba clubs of Rio or the boulevards of gay Par-ee?

"Oh," you say, "just throw a few things together that'll get you by in a swamp."

Naturally, she thinks you're kidding, even after she notices you laying in a supply of mosquito repellant and aquasocks. And when you finally usher her into the Victoria Falls Hotel, following a spine-numbing twenty-two-hour flight, she smiles simultaneously at the pleasing surroundings and what she believes was your little joke. The Vic Falls, perhaps the lone nineteenth-century colonial hotel still operating in southern Africa, may have a run or two in its safari stockings, a few stains on its bush jacket, but it's as romantic as the last act of a bad operetta.

Seedily luxurious, the low, rambling wings of the Vic Falls are tickled by palm fronds, scampered over by monkeys, serviced by an attentive staff in starched white livery, and moistened by mists from cataracts so immense they make Niagara seem like a leaky faucet. Your girlfriend is really settling into the place, especially its spacious patio, but the ice has hardly melted in her second gin-and-tonic before you've booked passage on Air Botswana, and toward the end of the next afternoon, the two of you are flying over territory that decidedly resembles . . . *swamp*. Vast, horizon-to-horizon swamp. You're made a trifle sad by the look she gives you.

For reasons that are typically African (where all the clocks have elastic hands and rubber faces), yet difficult to explain, the flight from Victoria Falls, Zimbabwe, to Maun, Botswana, arrives nearly two hours late, and as you wait for your luggage, the guide who has met you at the yam-patch airport is nervously glancing from his watch to the sky and back again. "We have a ways to go, and we've got to get there before dark," you explain to your companion. When she asks, "Suppose we don't?" you shrug. You're afraid of what she might answer if you inquire if she's ever spent the night with a slobbering beast.

Before long you're motorboating up a reedy, sullen river, exchanging waves with folks who've never so much as heard of George Bush, even though their relatives are Bushmen. Before you can think to congratulate them, they, their huts, and their goats have vanished, and your boat is alone on a waterway that twists through the aquatic flora like a spastic vegetarian through a salad bar, and whose banks are closing in on you from both sides. The river narrows into a channel. The channel into a hippopotamus path.

Meanwhile, the sun has slipped below the palm-fringed horizon and the temperature is dropping so fast you think it must have fallen off a cliff. It gets later and later, darker and darker, colder and colder, lonelier and lonelier, the route more and more crooked, the papyrus beds more and more dense, and your girlfriend has to pee so bad she must gnaw on her camera strap to stifle a howl.

Still, the emerging stars are flamboyant, the birdcalls crystalline, the frog din hypnotic, and the situation really isn't all that horrifying, considering how lost you appear to be.

Then you hit the WALL OF GNATS!

You call it a wall instead of a cloud because clouds don't usually give a person whiplash. You're talking about the force of trillions of tiny bugs per cubic foot here, gnat cheek to gnat jowl, and you're swallowing gnats and breathing gnats while *National Enquirer* headlines – couple drowns in gnat tsunami – dance before your gnat-blinded eyes. On you bore, meter after meter, into the LIVING WALL!, certain you're within a gnat's hair of asphyxiation, until the wall suddenly crumbles away as inexplicably as it materialized, and in the distance you glimpse a flicker of light that's of apparent human fabrication.

In ten minutes you're docked at Ntswi Island, a campfire and a beefy meal in your immediate future. Ah, but any illusion that things are now hunky-dory disappears when you discover that your girlfriend couldn't quite hold it until she reached the thatched latrine. There's nothing like wet pants to throw a wet blanket on swampland romance.

Add to that some loud-mouthed hippos reciting the Hippocratic oath a few-score yards from your tent, and the savage chill that is piercing your lightweight sleeping bag (in Botswana, mid-June has turned out to be midwinter: you'd think those people south of the equator could get their seasons straight), and you have a night that belongs to misery, not to Michelob. You greet the dawn with no more glee than your significantly silent sweetie.

Gradually, however, you warm to the place and it to you. Before the afternoon is over, the temperature will have hit eighty – a fifty-degree swing that occurs each day – and the sky will have pinned blue ribbons to every lapel of the Okavango delta, irrefutably a first-prize swamp.

The Okavango is the largest inland delta in the world. It's formed when the Okavango River, overfed by floodwaters from the rains of Angola, runs headlong into the Kalahari Desert, and skids to a stop without ever reaching the sea. The result is seventeen thousand square kilometers of channels, lagoons, reedbeds, grass pans, and islands. The water is pure enough to drink, warm enough to bathe in, although if you splash for more than ten minutes, a drooling crocodile will usually show up and demand a wine list. In a week, however, your party sees not one poisonous snake nor one squadron of bloodthirsty mosquitoes, lest anyone think to compare it with the Everglades. As for the WALL OF GNATS!, it seems to have gone the way of the walls of Jericho, the Iron Curtain, and a flasher's longjohns.

What you do see in this glistening oasis of water lilies, phoenix palms, and melapo grass are storks and fish eagles, hornbills and bee-eaters; you see parrots, vultures, lilac-breasted rollers, and literally hundreds of other ornithological showpieces. Everywhere, great wings beat the air as if it were a drum, and when the day chorus of doves and cuckoos punches off duty, the more esoteric night birds come on-line.

On the larger islands – and some are many times the size of Manhattan – there is game. Big game. Buffalo, giraffe, zebra, elephant, lion, leopard, et al.; most of the stereotypes of the African tableau, although they appear anything but stereotypical when you're stalking them on foot, and worrying if they might be stalking you. Hiking unarmed through acacia thornbush, in fairly close proximity to the wildest of animals, gives your Okavango experience that dark edge of danger without which romance is merely the sappy side of lust.

Tranquillity is also a necessary component of romantic adventure, and there's no shortage of peaceful epiphanies in this watery Eden. Early each morning, your party pushes off in dugout canoes hollowed out from the single trunks of sausage trees. Powered by a native guide with a twelve-foot pole, you glide noiselessly along the hippo paths, your bow knocking a shower of dew pearls from the papyrus tops, whiffs of nectar in the air, as all about you fin, fang, and feather receive the Day-Glo kiss of the slowly rising sun.

After a day of walking and marveling, you are poled back to tiny Ntswi Isle, where, at a primitive open-air bar decorated with skulls, that same sun, setting now, is reflected off cold cans of local beer. The dusk belongs to Lion Lager.

And one evening, sure enough, beneath the gloriously exotic configuration of the Southern Cross – it happens to be the night after a bull elephant drank the sudsy water in which your girlfriend had just washed out her underthings, an act that filled you with a perverse mixture of revulsion and jealousy – your paramour interrupts the Okavango concert of cricket and ibis and mystery beast to whisper, "Baby, it's a known fact that you've got depraved taste, but I think you may be right about this ol' swamp. It's the most romantic spot on earth."

Esquire, 1990

Note: Water with short grass growing in it is a bog. Water with tall grass growing in it is a marsh. Water with trees growing in it is a swamp. Technically, then, the Okavango delta is much more marsh than swamp. For failing to honor that distinction back in 1990, I now voluntarily surrender my poetic license for one year.

The Eight-Story Kiss

At a distance – and it can be seen from bridges and cause-ways more than a mile away – it seems to rise out of the sea, huge and rosy, like Godzilla in a prom dress: pretty in pink. And one can be forgiven for imagining that one is gazing at the single biggest, pinkest Big Pink thing on a planet where, admit-tedly, not many things manage to be simultaneously massive in scale and vivid of hue. At least, not of that hue normally asso-ciated with cotton candy, Pepto-Bismol, and girlie underwear.

I've never spent a night at the Don CeSar Resort Hotel in St. Petersburg Beach, Florida, but I've been there many times. I go there to lounge in the lobby, drink in the bar, wander the grounds, and partake of a Sunday seafood buffet that, as near as I can judge, is unequaled anywhere for bounty, variety, and flavor. Mostly, however, I go there to experience the pinkness.

There was a time when pink was the unofficial state color of Florida, a perfect chromatic complement to sunny skies, green palms, and turquoise waters. The luxurious Don CeSar, built in 1928 and periodically remodeled, is a proudly sur-viving relic of Old Florida, the paradisiacal, magnetic Florida that in the first half of the 20th century sweetened the dreams and warmed the fantasies of generations of snowbound Americans.

The hotel has its counterparts in Miami, to be sure, but

Miami is a *scene,* man; Miami is hip, whereas St. Pete Beach is so untrendy as to be genuinely cool. And the Don CeSar Hotel, along with what's left of the Everglades and the House of Prayer Bar-B-Cue in Ft. Lauderdale, is one of the most compelling reasons for visiting a tragically overdeveloped state that has far too many concealed weapons, far too few sane drivers, and that by and large has left its pink period behind it.

The Don CeSar's bar – embedded in the dim inner recesses of this citadel of tropical nostalgia like a coffee bean in a kilo of aspic – is the sort of place that inspires the consumption of strawberry margaritas. One afternoon there, I was even moved to quaff pink ladies, the favorite libation of pink-haired ladies who coif pink poodles, a breed of beast not entirely absent from the hotel's premises. In fact, the Don CeSar itself is kind of a pink poodle, although there's nothing really frou-frou about the resort. It doesn't sing out, "I'm cute," but rather, "I'm relaxed. I'm on permanent holiday alongside the Gulf of Mexico, I'm comfortable and happy-go-lucky and festive and affluent and free to be any damn color I choose to be, and I choose to be – PINK!"

Pink is what red looks like when it kicks off its shoes and lets its hair down. Pink is the boudoir color, the cherubic color, the color of Heaven's gates. (Not pearly or golden, brothers and sisters: *pink*.) Pink is as laid back as beige, but while beige is dull and bland, pink is laid back with *attitude*. The Don CeSar (275 rooms and all the water sports a bipedal mammal can handle) wears that attitude well. It knows that it looks as if it were carved out of bubblegum, as if it mutated from a radioactive conch patch, as if it leaked from the vat where old flamingos go to dye – but the Don CeSar doesn't care. It simply winks, lazily flaunts its pigmentation, and like a cartoon panther who's peddled its last lucrative roll of home insulation, turns its face to the sun.

Because pink, unique in the spectrum, is essentially para-doxical, the decorator's paint of choice for Mexican brothel and New England nursery, it's called upon to signify both naughtiness and innocence. Thus when I describe the Don CeSar as architecturally affectionate, a kind of structural kiss, I'm referring not only to hot and hungry honeymoon oscula-tion but to that chaste smooch a young Esther Williams used to blow to all the shivering northern masses just before she dove into a pellucid pool way back there in a more innocuous age.

In a different mood, I'm also inclined to think of the Don CeSar as shrimp cocktail for the eyes. And as long as it doesn't change color, I'll keep stopping by every year or so for a taste of it. Someday, I may go so far as to book a room there. You can tell it to the CIA, you can tell it to the FBI, you can tell it to Jerry Falwell and all the little Falwells: when it comes to beach hotels, comrades, I'm a dedicated pinko.

National Geographic Traveler, 2000

The Cannibal King Wants
His Din-Din

When the roosters that scratch in the yard of Brastagi's best hotel crowed me awake that steamy tropical dawn, I, personally, wasn't feeling all that cocky. In retrospect, however, I suppose I might be forgiven had I rolled out of bed with a bit of attitude because – believe it or not – before the Sumatran sun would set, I, an unassuming, modern, civilized commoner with a taste for donuts and garden vegetables, would be brandishing the savage scepter of a man-eating monarchy. That's right. Tom, King of the Cannibals!

The previous day had been interesting enough, much of it spent at a jungle outpost that functions as an orangutan rehabilitation center. No, no, Indonesia's population of big red apes isn't plagued by drug or alcohol problems, but some of the goofily beautiful animals (imagine Arnold Schwarzenegger crossed with Lucille Ball and the prototype for the Gerber Baby) do suffer an addiction of an even more dangerous sort. Captured as infants to be pets in the households of the rich, they develop a fondness for and a dependency on human companionship. When they grow too large and powerful to be any longer manageable around the house, the domesticated primates are turned over to a government agency that transports them to a wilding compound in the mountains where they're gradually taught to fend for themselves and be mistrustful of men. An excellent idea, of course, since every living thing on this planet, including men, would be wise to be mistrustful of men. But I digress.

My little group was in northwestern Sumatra to raft the Alas, a remote river that cuts through the rainforest with a silver track, offering a few thrilling rapids, but, most alluringly, daily opportunities to spy on truly wild orangutans and, if we were lucky, an Asian rhino or a tiger or two. (We tried not to consider possible encounters with cobras or kraits.)

An exploratory party from Sobek, the California-based adventure company, had accomplished the very first rafting of the Alas only months before, and we – eight paying passengers, four Sobek guides, and an Indonesian forest ranger who spent his spare time reading Louis L'Amour westerns – were to be the second rafters ever to run the strand.

So serenely did we conceal our nervous excitement that morning that we could have been compared to a bag of marshmallows at a Girl Scout camp. After nibbling at the hotel's advertised "American breakfast" (chilled fried eggs, diced papaya, and processed cheese), we hurried aboard a snub-nosed buslike vehicle of unknown manufacture to be driven to the spot deep in the leafy hills where we'd be putting our inflatable boats in the water.

Adventure travel is by definition unpredictable, however, and we never reached the Alas, alas, at least not that day. Instead, acting on a fortuitous tip from a Mobil Oil geologist that a rare daylong exhumation ceremony was about to unfold in an isolated village of the Karo Batak tribe, we detoured, parallel-parked between two water buffalo, and, following the oilman's crude map, hiked five miles into an anthropologist's dream.

Aside from the occasional oil explorer, timber cruiser, or

misguided Christian missionary, the Karo Batak had never been exposed to blue-eyed devils. Yet, when – blue eyes as wide as poker chips – our foreign mob suddenly appeared out of nowhere, we were received as honored guests. So gracious was their hospitality, in fact, that after a confab, tribal leaders declared that a pair from our group would be crowned king and queen for the day.

Being both very strong and very sweet, the guide Beth was a logical choice for queen. Why they chose me as their king I haven't a clue. Certainly it had nothing to do with my literary reputation, although some novelists are known to practice *verbal* cannibalism, biting and gnawing on one another insatiably at cocktail parties or in reviews.

At any rate, our hosts escorted Beth and me to sexually segregated longhouses where they wrapped us in regal sarongs and other colorful raiments and hung about thirty pounds of solid gold jewelry – the village treasury – from our respective necks and appendages. (They must have figured we were too weighted down to skip town.)

There was then a royal procession back to the principal longhouse, where now on display were the remains of seven persons recently exhumed from the graves where they'd lain for years while their families saved enough money to fund the ceremony that would finally usher their spirits into the Karo Batak version of heaven. The bones were lovingly washed, dried, and stacked in seven neat piles, a skull atop each pile like some kind of Halloween cherry. Then the celebration began.

Beth disappeared into a shadowy corner where she remained for hours (afraid, perhaps, that her regal counterpart might demand his conjugal rights?), but my "subjects" and I commenced to dance ritualistically around those graveyard sundaes. Danced around them and around them and around them. Energized by betel nut, the chewing of which stained my numb mouth the color of Buck Rogers's rocketship, and inspired by two talented groups of drummers and snake-charmer flute tooters, I managed to learn the proper repetitive steps and to tirelessly dance the day away.

Now, to be quite truthful, the Karo Batak appeared innocently tame and, despite periodic reports to the contrary, are believed not to have lunched upon any of their fellows in about four generations. Many are Christian (leading me to wonder if they might especially enjoy Holy Communion: that is, "swallow the leader"). Nevertheless, when toward evening an unappetizing zombie-gray stew was served, we intruders politely excused ourselves – as an abdicating monarch, I shook every hand in the village – and took the long muddy trek back to our bus.

At the very worst, the stew meat was dog, and probably it had come from upcountry cousins of those Hotel Brastagi roosters who had cock-a-doodled our reveille. Be that as it may, I shall never cease to insist that once upon a time, in the tiger-haunted hills of Sumatra, I reigned as King of the Cannibals. And at those who might dispute that claim, I'm fully prepared to hurl the ancient and traditional curse of the Karo Batak: "I pick the flesh of your relatives from between my teeth."

The New York Times Magazine, 1986

The Day the Earth Spit Warthogs

The first time I was bitten by a tsetse fly (Ouch! Son of a bitch! Those suckers *hurt*!), I was convinced that in days, if not hours, I would be nodding out, snoring on the job, dreaming at the switch, yawning like a heavy-metal rocker stranded in Salt Lake City, just another droopy victim of the dreaded and sorrowful "sleeping sickness."

During my two weeks in the Selous, my tender flesh was subsequently stabbed, my vintage blood swilled by at least forty tsetse flies, so far without dire consequence – although I must confess that as I begin this report, I'm starting to feel a teeny bit drowsy. Should I doze off in the middle of a sentence (an experience probably not uncommon to some of my readers), I want it known there's no regrets. The lethal lullaby of an infected tsetse (the most romantically named of all flies) is arguably preferable to the anesthetic drone of computers, freeway traffic, and television sets; and the wild, hot beauty of the Selous is worth almost any risk.

* * * * * * * * * *

The Selous is the largest uninhabited game reserve in the world. Located in central Tanzania, a couple of hundred miles south of Mount Kilimanjaro, the Selous is no national park

TOM ROBBINS

where tourists sprawl on rattan sofas, sipping gin and listening to the BBC as from the air-conditioned safety of posh lodges they spy shamelessly on mating lions. In the Selous, one doesn't catch a safari bus to the corner of Zebra and Watusi. To see the Selous, one hikes and one paddles. And when an aggravated hippopotamus is charging one's rubber raft, one paddles very hard, indeed.

When I announced to family and friends that I was going hiking and river rafting through a vast patch of African cabbage, they didn't ask why. They must have realized that after three years bent over an idling and backfiring novel, skinning my knuckles on every bolt and wrench in the literary toolbox, I needed to blow a little carbon out of my own exhaust. Perhaps they also sensed that after my recent dealings with editors, agents, lawyers, producers, and reviewers, I might be primed for the company of crocodiles.

Nobody was particularly concerned that I was off to walk with the animals, talk with the animals, squawk with the animals. After all, I once turned down an offer of manatee steak in a weird restaurant in Cuba, and I have made it a life-long practice never to date women who wear leopard-skin pillbox hats. My beast karma was pretty good.

Nevertheless, having heard AMA terror stories of schisto-somiasis and malaria, of elephantiasis-enlarged testicles so huge the poor owner has to push them around in a wheel-barrow, and yes, of the narcoleptic legacy of the tsetse fly, family and friends fretted one and all about tropical disease. Apparently, the evident scares us less than the invisible: we figure it's easier to outrun a bear than a bugbear.

Well, folks, not to worry. First, I was stuffed to the gullet with malaria prophylactics and pincushioned with inocula-tions against the most prevalent tropical maladies (unfortu-nately, there's no [yawn] serum that wards off "sleeping sickness"), and second, the very fact that the Selous is unoc-

50

cupied by humans or farm animals means disease is rarely con-
tracted there. In the Selous, the tsetse is all pester and no
siesta. *Ah,* but I'd overlooked one thing. The Selous *itself* is a
tropical disease: feverish, lethargic, exotic, achy, sweaty, hallucinogenic, and, as I've learned since coming home, recurrent.

Just when I think that I'm over it, that rush-hour gridlock,
income-tax audits, and two viewings of *Amadeus* have
worked their acculturizing cures, I suffer yet another attack of
Selous flu. It comes on with a humid vapor, with a vibration
of membrane, with howls and hoofbeats that nobody else in
the room can hear, and although I might be in the midst of
something truly important, such as choosing which brand of
burglar alarm to install on my newly violated front door, it
never fails to distract me with memories of a sweeter, cleaner,
if less comfortable place; a place where clocks dissolve, where
even death is honest, and primitive equalities prevail. . . .

* * * * * * * * * * *

It's our first day in the bush. At this point, I'm still a tsetse
virgin. From the port city of Dar es Salaam, we have traveled
into the interior on a toy railroad: one locomotive, one car,
and narrow-gauge track, all three built by the Chinese. It was
definitely not a main line. It was a chow mein line.

Okay, okay, but the chow on the train *was* pretty good. We
bought it through our windows at brief village stops. There
were cashew nuts, absolute state-of-the-art mangoes, and
thumb-size bananas that melted in our mouths. Prices were so
cheap they made us feel like muggers.

During the five-hour rail trip, we'd gotten acquainted with
our leaders, employees of Sobek Expeditions, a company of,
well, reasonably sane adventurers from Angels Camp,
California. The Sobek people had chased thrills, chills, and
spills all over the globe, but they were as excited as the rest of

us when, halfway into the ride, we began to spot a few animals: a baboon here, a warthog there, a small herd of distant bushbuck, and in the ponds and marshes (lavendered with water lilies the color of Oscar Wilde's hankies) yellow-billed storks taller than most Little League second basemen, poised there among the lily pads as if waiting for a throw from center field.

Yes, it was exciting, but there was a bit of a theme-park atmosphere about it as well; as if those random creatures had been placed in our field of vision by a San Diego entrepreneur. Then, suddenly, a pair of giraffes bounced into view. When the engineer mischievously sounded his whistle, the giraffes panicked. Stiff stilts churning, necks waving like rubber bands, they bolted toward rather than away from us, and in their confusion very nearly crashed into the side of our car. One wheeling giraffe was so close I could have flipped a cashew into its terrified muzzle. Oh, Boy! Oh, Cheetah! Oh, Tarzan and Jane! This was Africa, baby, this was the real thing! But it was not yet the Selous.

* * * * * * * * * * *

Our first day in the bush finds us up at dawn. Having only seen dawn from the other side of the clock, I never imagined daybreak might actually be pleasant. The tsetselike sting of 5:00 a.m. is softened by the sight of an elephant family, Mom, Dad, Bud, and Sis, carelessly mashing a million dewdrops as they jumbo down a deep green valley to a water hole.

We watch the elephants from the rustic veranda of the Stiegler's Gorge Safari Camp, the last outpost of humanity we'll enjoy before we venture into the Selous. We had slept at the camp, or rather, *tried* to sleep, for an all-night newsboy choir of hyenas periodically sang us awake. Late the previous afternoon, the train had deposited us at a village called Fuga, the end of the line, where we – eighteen of us, including the guides – were met by a trio of Land Rovers and driven for a couple of battering hours down an Armageddon of a road, a moonscape of a lane to Stiegler's Gorge. By the time our gear was stowed in our respective huts, it was dark and a rusty gong had summoned us to a dinner of green beans and steak.

Dave, a veteran guide, had hoisted a morsel of that steak aloft in the lanternshine. "Impala," he had said authoritatively, studying his fork. "At first I thought it might be sable. Africa is an adventure in meat."

At any rate, it's our first morning in the bush, and a detachment of us hike for three hours from the Stiegler's Gorge complex, beneath a blue sky that's already hissing like a blowtorch. Down in Tanzania, it's July in January, and if the sun has anything to say about it, there's a fireworks display all day, every day.

The savanna grass is green but dry, and it crunches underfoot. J'nanga, our native game guide, steps noiselessly on the bare patches between clumps of grass, but we cement-footed Americans sound as if we're breakdancing in a silo of Rice Krispies. Our gauche sneakers scuff at fresh cheetah tracks, at shiny licorice drops of wildebeest dung, at impala skulls as bleached as a surfer's eyebrows, at midget wildflowers, and a mega-Manhattan of ants.

Scattered about the plain are trees that resemble huge stone jars; trees that resemble dendritic delicatessens festooned with salami and pepperoni; trees that appear to be growing upside down; trees that look like 50s haircuts, their foliage organically barbered into Sha Na Na flattops; and – outnumbering all the rest – leafless trees bristling with thorns so long and sharp they could pierce the heart of a bureaucrat.

The trees, the flowers, even the piles of gnu poo are attended by butterflies, some as tiny and yellow as buttercup petals, others as big as pie tins and colored like Shanghai silk.

There are also a great many bees. They're not killer bees, but we haven't learned that yet, and it is while fending off one of these buzzers that Flo falls, cameras and all, into a warthog burrow.

Warthogs aren't killers, either, except maybe when cornered, but with their curved tusks and flatiron faces, they look like the nightmares of a lapsed Jew who's just had his first bite of ham. The steel-wool warthog, not pink Porky, is the pig that ought to have the job of announcing "That's all, folks!" Who'd argue? On another game walk, a week later, seven of these fearsome swine suddenly came barreling, one by one, out of a deep burrow that we were innocently passing, nearly knocking the pins from under a startled Yvonne and planting the fear of the Ultimate Bacon in each of us. On our calendars, that day became known as The Day the Earth Spit Warthogs, and Yvonne, for one, will probably devote January 21 to prayer and fasting for the rest of her life.

On this, our first day in the bush, there are no pigs at home, however, and nothing is bruised except Flo's dignity. It is while she's brushing herself off that J'nanga sights a herd of buffalo.

There are about two hundred of them, weighing in at three tons each (and it doesn't take Ronald McDonald's calculator to figure that that's a whole lot of McBuffalo burgers). Fortunately, we're downwind of the herd, so we're able to move within forty yards of it before we're noticed.

There's a large fallen tree in our vicinity, and J'nanga directs us into its dead branches. We watch the buffalo and they watch us. It's difficult to tell who's more nervous. The mature bulls station themselves at the perimeter of the herd, glowering with almost tangible menace. They paw the ground and snort short Hemingway sentences, resonant with ill will.

J'nanga is thinking he might have made a mistake. The Cape buffalo, rotten-tempered, heavy of hoof and horn, is among Africa's most dangerous animals, and here he's gone and got a half-dozen honkies treed by a herd that could reduce Grand Central Station to gravel. The buffalo are indisposed to retreat, and we seem to have lost that option.

Jim, an environmentalist cowboy attorney accustomed to stalking Sierra sheep, grinds happily away with his video camera while J'nanga ponders the situation. In Jim's ear, I whisper, *"Hatari!"* I suspect Jim has seen more John Wayne movies than I, but if he remembers Wayne's 1962 film and recognizes the Swahili word for "danger," he doesn't let on. "Big *hatari*!" I whisper. He goes on videoing.

It's hot enough in our tree to broil escargot, and even our daredevil guides are beginning to see mirages. Over there to the left: is that a grove of thorn trees or a Club Med swimming pool? Perhaps J'nanga is getting light-headed, too. He commences to whistle, shrilly, through his fingers, as if at a babe in a bikini. At the sound, the buffalo stage a semistampede. They thunder to a spot beyond the phantom tanning beds, a good eighty yards away, before stopping to resume their Cold War diplomacy.

Taking immediate advantage of this partial withdrawal, J'nanga hustles us out of the tree and, covering us with his rifle, dispatches us toward a low hill – on the opposite side of which, a few minutes later, we are charged by an adolescent elephant.

Between meals, as well as at table, Africa is, indeed, an adventure in meat.

* * * * * * * * * * *

The next morning, the real fun begins. Bleary-eyed from the insomnolent effects of hyena serenade, we put our rafts in the water and paddle into the Selous. For the next two weeks, we'll see no other humans, just animals, birds, fang-snapping reptiles – and, of course, the gods of the river.

Sobek employees are quite familiar with river gods. Anybody who does much rafting gets to recognize the invisible deities who rule each particular river, sometimes each particular rapid in a river. The very name "Sobek" is borrowed from the crocodile god of the Nile. It was chosen as both a charm and an homage.

Rivers are the true highways of life. They transport the ancient tears of disappeared races, they propel the foams that will impregnate the millennium. In flood or in sullen repose, the river's power cannot be overestimated, and only men modernized to the point of moronity will be surprised when rivers eventually take their revenge on those who dam and defile them. River gods, some muddy, others transparent, ride those highways, singing the world's inexhaustible song.

In terms of white water, the Rufiji, the river that drains the Selous, is a pussycat. Once free of the confines of Stiegler's Gorge, it hums a barely audible refrain. *Ah*, but though the gods of the Rufiji are fairly silent gods, we are soon to learn that their mouths are open wide.

Actually, the Rufiji is part of a river *system*. As it approaches the Indian Ocean it separates into channel after channel, forming a plexus of waterways so confusing no explorer has quite been able to map it. At one point it vanishes into the palm swamps of Lake Tagalala, only to slither out on the eastern side like a many-headed serpent.

Through Stiegler's Gorge, the Rufiji gives us a fine fast spin, comparable, say, to the waves of the Rogue, if not the Colorado. One rapid, in fact, is so rowdy that our cargo-rigged Avon rafts dare not challenge it; thus, less than an hour after we've put in, we're involved in a laborious portage.

A few miles downstream, the Rufiji takes its foot off the accelerator, never to speed again. It just grows lazier and slower until there's virtually no current at all. Deprived of the luxury of drift, we're forced to paddle the entire distance –

forty-five steamy miles – to our take-out point. Moreover, the rafts are so heavily loaded with equipment (including Jim's four video cameras) and supplies (including Chicago Eddie's starched white tennis outfits and gold chains) that it requires a marathon of muscling to move them along.

None of us passengers is an Olympic paddler, exactly, and the guides might have had to provide more than their share of the locomotion were it not for the impetus of hippopotamus. Every languorous labyrinth of the Rufiji is choked with hippos, and for a full fortnight those lardy torpedoes were to dominate our lives.

There're plenty of crocodiles, chartreuse and ravenous, in the Rufiji as well, but like the CIA, the crocs are funded for covert actions only. Camouflaged and stealthy, crocs are masters of the sneak attack. The nastiness of hippos is magnificently blatant.

Apparently, among animals as among human beings, we entertain misconceptions about who are the good guys and who are the villains. The horned rhinoceros, for example, enjoys a public reputation equivalent to that, say, of a Hell's Angel. "Lock up the children, Elizabeth! Big *hatari*!" The hippo, on the other hand, having been filmed in frilly tutus by Disney, its gross grin having been cutie-pied by a thousand greeting-card artists, is regarded as affectionately as a jovial fat boy.

Basically, however, the rhino is a quiet, shy, gentle creature. Sure, it will halfheartedly charge a Land Rover, but that's because its eyesight is so poor it mistakes the vehicle for another rhino, with whom it would mate or spar. Like many a biker, the rhino is mainly just out for a good time. The hippo, on the other hand, is loud, hostile, and aggressive. Extremely territorial, it pursues with fury anything audacious enough to encroach upon its neighborhood. Nothing, neither lion nor leopard, python nor crocodile, will tangle with a hippo. The unattractive rhino is the victim of bad press. The cherubic hippo kills more people every year than any other animal in Africa.

When we discover rhino tracks one day, on a plain a few miles from Lake Tagalala, our native guides literally jump for joy. They had believed all rhinos gone from the Selous, destroyed by poachers, who market the powdered horn to Oriental businessmen with waning sex drives. Conversely, we paddle past a hundred hippos daily, not one of whom offers us anything but trouble.

Cries of "Hippo right!" or "Hippo left!" ring out every few minutes from the guides. Should one of the surprisingly swift monsters prove particularly threatening, a guide slaps the water with his paddle, making a resounding *swak!* that, being an unfamiliar sound, frequently will halt a charge, at least temporarily. Meanwhile, everybody else in the raft paddles as if his or her life depends on it.

When we put into shore for lunch or to camp for the night, we're exhausted. Panting, arms aching, percolating in our own perspiration, we stumble from the rafts and flop down in the nearest shade. It's Miller time, right? Wrong. No beer, no ice. The refreshment we're served is Rufiji punch: raspberry Kool-Aid made with river water that has been purified via medicine kit. The water is eighty degrees, buzzing with silt, stinking of iodine, and no doubt heavily laced with crocodile drool and hippo pee. We welcome it as if it were French champagne.

Characteristically, hippopotamuses make a noise that is a cross between scales being run on an out-of-tune bassoon and the chortling of a mad Roman emperor. Throughout the night, we are treated to their ruckus. The guides say that the hippos, being nocturnal feeders, are protesting because we've set up our tents in their dining room. Personally, I think they're making fun of us for the way we guzzle that punch.

Our food is a James Beard–size improvement over our beverage. Under very crude conditions our guides manage to turn out delicious spaghetti, chop suey, and, amazingly, banana crepes flambé. (Have the native guides any doubt that we Americans are crazy, it vanishes as they watch, eyes wide with horror, as Dave sets fire to a quantity of perfectly good rum.) True, toward the end of the journey, supplies running thin, we might fantasize about one of those little osterias where, with a smear of garlic and a squirt of wine, an Italian can make a dead fish sing like a nightingale. But we haven't come to the Selous to eat and drink.

Even were there restaurants in the Selous, the cuisine of greater Tanzania consists primarily of *ugali*, a pasty dough that is torn into pieces with the fingers and dunked in sauce. Sauce d'impala, sauce de sable, sauce de dik-dik, sauce de flying termite. An adventure in meat. And although there are sweltering moments when I'd gladly trade my firstborn child for a frosty bottle of Safari Lager, that brand of beer, the only one available in Tanzania, is no gold-medal winner.

No, we haven't come to the Selous to wine and dine, nor to sightsee and shop. We've come to seek an audience with the river gods, to show ourselves to them and accept their banishment or their boons. We've come to test ourselves against water dragons with ears like wads of hairy bubblegum and gaping yawns like a thousand cases of "sleeping sickness" rolled into one. We've come to the Selous to outrace the hippos.

Did I say that we are exhausted at the conclusion of our morning and afternoon paddles? True, we're tired, but we're also exhilarated. We're so elated our bones are practically singing in their weary sockets, and, narrow escapes or not, it is with *eagerness* that we wrap ourselves against the homicidal sun and go out on the river again.

Because of the naughty habits of the crocodiles, we're forced to bathe onshore, showering with buckets of muddy water drawn cautiously from the stream. Now, Chicago Eddie might whine that he'd rather be soaking in a marble tub in some fancy hotel, but nobody really believes him. The Rufiji pantheon, lurid of feather, strong of tooth, has tripped an ancient wire in Eddie's cells, and, like the other seventeen of us, he broadcasts secret signals of ecstasy – Radio Eden – as, gold chains swinging, he penetrates ever deeper into the Selous.

* * * * * * * * * *

Perhaps it would be helpful could I inform you that the Selous is the size of Rhode Island with a crust of Connecticut tossed in. Unfortunately, such facts are not at my disposal. My East African guidebook contained that sort of information, but I lent it to a fellow rafter and it was never returned. She hints that when our supplies ran low, she'd boiled it for breakfast; talk about your adventure in meat. That same woman also claims to be watched over by the ghost of her recently deceased dog, Juliet, and that it's this spectral poodle, rather than guides and gods, who's steering us safely through the hippos. That's the kind of lady Kitty is, and I, for one, am happy she's along.

All I can report is that the Selous is extensive, its wildlife density is astonishing, and if its heart (a heart of brightness, to contradict Conrad) is invaded by other than scattered poachers, the annual Sobek expeditions, and an infrequent government inspection team, the evidence is missing. We meet strange insects here, including a sort of miniature science-fiction flying fortress as glossy black as Darth Vader's mascara, with long, thick, school-bus-yellow antennae, but there isn't a trace of litterbug.

The Selous is savanna: short-grass, middle-grass, and tall-grass savanna. Some of the plains seem almost manicured, so meticulously have they been mowed by the mouths of munching herds. The green hills roll like surf into a distance, where they turn slowly to purple. From Tagalala on to the sea, elegant palms line the various banks of the river. Occasionally we come upon a Tarzan-esque glade, complete with pool and vines.

Johnny Weissmuller, the consummate movie Tarzan, was the tallest hero of my boyhood, and more often during my life than is socially acceptable I've been moved to imitate his famous yell. To some, the Tarzan yodel is corny, campy, childish, and vulgar. To me, it's more stirring than the bravest battle cry, more glorious than the loftiest operatic aria, more profound than the most silvery outpouring of oratory. The Tarzan yell is *the* exultant cry of man the innocent, man the free. It warbles back and forth across the boundary between human and beast, expressing in its extremes and convolutions all the unrestrained and holy joy of ultimate aliveness.

In the past, unfortunately, I've usually bounced my Tarzan yells off the insensitive ears of cocktail-lounge commandos, invariably attracting the wrong kind of attention. Here, at last, in the glades of the Selous, it is released in proper context. It gives me that old Weissmuller Saturday-matinee primal chill as it comes quavering out of my throat to mix in the Selous twilight with the smoker's coughs of a distant pride of lions, the spooky erotic murmurs of a treeful of waking bats, and that ceaseless, ubiquitous pulsebeat of body Africana, the echoing hoot of the emerald-throated wood dove.

Our last day in the Selous is structured much like the others: up at dawn for a game walk into the bush, breakfast, break camp, two hours on the river, lunch, rest, two more hours playing Dodg'em car with the hippos, set up camp, another game walk before dark, dinner, bed. At the end of such a day, one requires no tsetse injection to speed one's slumber. On this final eve, however, many of us lie conscious, listening, holding on to every note of the ninety-piece orchestra of the African night. It is as if we dread the morning and our return to what we moderns like to think of as "civilization."

I'll bet that Chicago Eddie, supine amidst his ruined tennis whites in the adjacent tent, is recalling the impalas we had seen that dusk, crossing a narrow ridge single file, so that we could count them the way a child at a railroad crossing will sometimes count boxcars. Incidentally, there were exactly sixty-five of them silhouetted against the setting sun.

And I venture that Kathy, an erudite woman with a library of wildlife manuals in her knapsack, is still puzzling over the blank stare the aging guide M'sengala had given her when she'd asked whether the rare hartebeest we'd spotted was Lichtenstein's hartebeest or one of the other varieties. After that, M'sengala cracked up every time Jim and I inquired if we were looking at Rauschenberg's wildebeest. Rosenquist's bushbuck. Wesselman's waterbuck. Catskill's borschtbuck. Or Goldberg's variations. Knowing not ten words of English, he couldn't possibly savvy the cultural references, but M'sengala got the point.

Certainly M'sengala, with his goofy, infectious laugh, is in *my* thoughts. I'm remembering how shocked he'd looked when Curt had slipped the Sony Walkman headset over his leathery ears and turned up Huey Lewis and the News, and how quickly he'd begun to grin and then to dance, as if he could not stop himself from dancing. M'sengala got down! The Selous, itself, gets down. Down to basics, to the curious if natural rhythms of life.

And death. For if there's abundant life in the Selous, there's abundant death as well. We'd seen a pack of wild dogs cripple and devour an impala; a bloated hippo corpse being ripped to shreds by twenty crocodiles; the remains of a feline-butchered wildebeest, black clouds of flies buzzing like paparazzi around its instant celebrity of blood. We could hear those flies from thirty yards away.

Yes, there are ongoing dramas of death in the Selous, but except for the small amount imported by poachers, there's no unnecessary violence, no greed, no cruelty. Nor is there politics, religion, trendiness, ambition, hype, or sales pitch. Perhaps it's the very purity of the Selous that makes us cling to it, reluctant to let go.

For two weeks, we have traveled in the realm of the eternal. There is escape from the prison of the past, disinterest in the promise of the future. There is no other place. The Selous is *here*. There is no other time. The Selous is *now*.

And as we lie in our tents on the grassy plain of eternity it must occur to each and every one of us that the Selous is the way the world was meant to be – and that everything else is a mistake.

Nonetheless, we do return to carpeted home and electronic hearth, and I have to tell you, folks, now that I'm back, I'm ready for a nap. If it should prove that a tsetse fly has, indeed, drugged my vital fluids, then, O river gods, grant me a graceful fall into the sleep of the Selous. The bright slumber of Africa. The snooze of Kilimanjaro.

Esquire, 1985

TRIBUTES

The Doors

As clueless as Rome before the barbarians stormed its gates, as oblivious as Pompeii on the eve of Vesuvius's genocidal belch, Seattle was totally unprepared for the rape and pillage to which its youth were subjected at Eagles Auditorium last night. Neither was it ready for the anointment, the empowerment, or the sanctification that were also part and parcel of a rock concert cum psychic ordeal cum full-blown ecstasy rite.

For some time now, Seattle's adopted "house" bands have been The Youngbloods and Country Joe & the Fish, groups whose electrical bananas may shock straight society but who, to their fans, are as folksy and affectionate as psychedelic puppies. Accustomed to having their faces licked, Seattleites were caught off guard by a band that, while it might sniff a crotch or two, definitely does not wag its tail; by a band that embodies the prevailing zeitgeist, with all of its political optimism, spiritual awareness, and liberating transcendence of obsolete values, but embodies it with an unprecedented potency, concentration, and theatrical vehemence; a band that flaunts rather than soft-pedals the threat that the new culture presents to the old culture – and that leaves both cultures rather reeling from the experience.

When, dazed but fomented, we staggered at last from the hall last night, we were each and every one under the spell of four musicians who, innocuously enough, call themselves after simple, ubiquitous, utilitarian devices intended for the closing off or opening up of architectural spaces.

Yes, that would be doors. But, my God, what doors are these?! Imagine jeweled glass panels, knobs that resemble spitting phalluses, mail slots that glow like jack-o'-lantern lips – and not a welcome mat in sight. Enter if you dare, my children, exit if you can.

The Doors. Their style is early cunnilingual, late patricidal, lunchtime in the Everglades, Black Forest blood sausage on electrified bread, Jean Genet up a totem pole, artists at the barricades, Edgar Allan Poe drowning in his birdbath, Massacre of the Innocents, tarantella of the satyrs, bacchanalian, Dionysian, L.A. pagans drawing down the moon.

The Doors. The musical equivalent of a ritual sacrifice, an amplified sex throb, a wounded yet somehow elegant yowl for the lost soul of America, histrionic tricksters making hard cider from the apples of Eden while petting the head of the snake.

The Doors. The intensity begins the moment they stalk on stage and it doesn't let up until the purge is over, the catharsis complete. Even between numbers, there is no relaxation: no chit-chat, no pandering, no horsing around. Like the classical actors of Japan, The Doors project all the more intensity when they are silent. They even tune up with an involvement so fierce it would scare The Mamas & The Papas out of their mama pants and papa pants.

The Doors. Their voice is dark and bloody, a voice from the bowels. Satanic in combustion, devouring in energy, awesome in spirit. The voice of Nietzsche, stopped short in terror, succumbing to madness, lusting for the salvation of flesh. The Brechtian voice of the Berlin Music Hall, warning a new generation of the rising tide of American fascism. A voice soaked with a rabid rage of destruction – yet neither wanton nor negative. Like Shiva, the Divine Destroyer of the Hindu, The Doors kill only to clear the way for rebirth; they evoke the eternal rhythmic balance of life and death, darkness and light – because the doors that really matter always swing both ways.

Four Doors:

John Densmore, drums. Perhaps the best drummer in all of rock. While most drummers seldom stray from the beat, Densmore crosses the beat – in and out, back and forth, creating counter-beats and accentuating the off-beats. He not only provides The Doors with a fantastic complexity of percussion, he goads them into new time signatures and actually leads them along their epic melodic line.

Ray Manzarek, organ. As authoritative as the Grateful Dead's Pigpen, but far more sophisticated, he obviously cut his teeth on Bach. Manzarek flows through a field of variations and figurations as grandiose as the richest Baroque. One moment he is pliant and searching, the next he is tearing at the keyboard like a starving man ripping a chicken apart.

Robby Krieger, guitar. With the drums and organ taking the lead, Krieger supplies a hard, unyielding rhythm that occasionally explodes into startling new disclosures of chord and modulation.

Jim Morrison, vocals. Morrison begins where Mick Jagger and Eric Burdon leave off. An electrifying combination of an angel in grace and a dog in heat, he becomes intoxicated by the danger of his poetry, and, swept by impious laughter, he humps the microphone, beats it, sucks it off. Sexual in an almost psychopathic way, Morrison's richly textured voice taunts and teases, threatens and throbs. With incredible vocal control and the theatrical projection of a Shakespearean star, he plays with the audience's emotions like a mischievous child with its dolls: now I kiss you, my little ones, now I wring your necks.

The Doors are carnivores in a land of musical vegetarians.

Their craftsmanship is all the more astonishing in the light of their savagery. They have the ensemble tightness of the Juilliard String Quartet – but their grandeur is not of the intellect but of warm red blood. Their stained talons, wet fangs, and leathery wings are seldom out of view, yet if they leave us crotch-raw and exhausted, at least they leave us aware of our aliveness. And of our destiny. The Doors scream into the darkened auditorium what all of us in the counterculture are whispering more softly in our hearts: We want the world and we want it . . . . NOW!

The Helix, 1967

Nurse Duffy of MTV

Her name sounds like one of those blue-collar taverns frequented by sports goons and off-duty cops, her job title sounds like the end of World War II. But Karen Duffy – the reigning "VJ" – looks more like an erotic bakery specializing in anatomically correct cream puffs, and her workplace looks more like the end of the world. As we know it. And she feels . . . fairly mischievous.

Coming at us in short bursts – Stella by strobelight – Duff manages nevertheless to be funny, bright, vulnerable, and genuine; the girl next door as video vamp, the perfect counterpoint to the laser-and-leather looney bin of MTV, over which she so jauntily presides.

Whether she is spinning Aerosmith's propeller or tossing MC Hammer his tacks, she introduces the optic sizzle, the hip-hop histrionics, as if she were Little Red Riding Hood showing off her pet wolves. She has bravado to spare, but her whip is licorice, her nerves just a bit on edge. (Van Halen, what sharp teeth you have!)

If MTV is simultaneously decadent and fresh, technologically sophisticated and emotionally primitive, both an accomplice to the apocalypse and its antidote, then who better than a former recreational therapist at a nursing home to reign over its sphere of paradoxical power? With alley-cat eyes, *pâtisserie* figure, Cubistic haircut, and a grin wide enough to put Julia Roberts's cat out through, Karen Duffy is capable of playing succubus to a generation of alienated young men. She is equally suited to be every patient's favorite candy striper in the rehab wards of a poisoned land.

So let's doff to Duff, let's quaff to Duff: a juicy burr under the stiff saddle of American puritanism; a witty companion in many a lonely, cathode-lit room; the reassuring wink at the center of a billion-dollar 'round-the-clock hallucination spawned by the uneasy marriage of commerce and art.

Esquire, 1992

Joseph Campbell

One humid, hammer-heavy morning seven years ago, on the ceremonial grounds of Chichen Itza, I watched a small coral snake slither from a pile of Mayan rubble and shoot through the grass like a rubber arrow in the direction of a group of my traveling companions. The snake singled out one man from the group, crawled deliberately up to the toe of his conservative, urban shoe, paused there for a long moment, then veered sharply to the right and disappeared into another heap of ancient stones.

That tiny incident would have been mildly interesting at best had not the man whom the snake "visited" been Joseph Campbell.

Professor Campbell had been regaling our party with some story or other, and gave no indication of having even noticed the little serpent. Yet I was convinced that something had passed between them.

Did the snake lick the tip of Joseph Campbell's shoelace, changing it into jade?

Was the snake carrying a tarot card under its tongue? Was it carrying a pomegranate seed?

Had the snake wept? Had it sung? Were those purple feathers sprouting from its spine?

Would the serpent and Professor Campbell meet again late

that evening – and would they sip mistletoe gin from a virgin's skull while discussing details for the coronation of the Ant King?

Speculations such as those were hardly surprising. Joseph Campbell was so conversant with the world of wonders that he awakened the potential for wonder in everyone he touched. He unbuttoned the secret earth for us and let the inexhaustible inspiration of Being stream through.

Now, like heroes before him, he has vanished into the buttonhole. But he left the bright opening agape, allowing us free access to that heritage of raptures and terrors that he so valiantly resurrected, so vividly described.

In the months before his death last year at the age of eighty-three, Campbell was interviewed at length by journalist Bill Moyers. The result, a six-part series entitled *Joseph Campbell and the Power of Myth,* is set to premiere on PBS later this month. It's virtually impossible to overestimate the significance of this suite of hour-long broadcasts, or to overpraise its potential for, temporarily at least, exorcising the boob from the tube. It's particularly significant at a time when the population is threatened by a potentially deadly epidemic of mythological origin. The plague to which I refer is not AIDS but millennialism.

Joseph Campbell was the world's foremost mythologist. Early in his long life, he combined Sir James George Frazer's discovery that strikingly similar motifs show up in the folktales of all the world's cultures, with Carl Jung's notion that myths are metaphors created to illuminate human experience. Thus, doubly inspired, Campbell became a maverick scholar, his books and lectures often scorned by academicians but adored by poets, painters, and enlightened psychoanalysts. His genius was not so much in his exhaustive scholarship, however, as in his intuitive recognition of the importance and relevance of myth to every living soul.

If "the proper study of man is man," then mythology is the lens through which man is properly examined. Yet most of us, including the ostensibly well-educated, wouldn't know a myth from a Pentagon press release. We've been taught to equate "myth" with "lie."

In actuality, myths are neither fiction nor history. Nor are most myths – and this will surprise some people – an *amalgamation* of fiction and history. Rather, a myth is something that never happened but is always happening. Myths are the plots of the psyche. They are ongoing, symbolic dramatizations of the inner life of the species, external metaphors for internal events.

As Campbell used to say, myths come from the same place dreams come from. But because they're more coherent than dreams, more linear and refined, they are even more instructive. A myth is the song of the universe, a song that, if accurately perceived, explains the universe and our often confusing place in it.

It is only when it is allowed to crystallize into "history" that a myth becomes useless – and possibly dangerous. For example, when the story of the resurrection of Jesus is read as a symbol for the spiritual rebirth of the individual, it remains alive and can continually resonate in a vital, inspirational way in the modern psyche. But when the resurrection is viewed as historical fact, an archival event that occurred once and only once, some two thousand years ago, then its resonance cannot help but flag. It may proffer some vague hope for our own immortality, but to our deepest consciousness it's no longer transformative or even very accessible on an everyday basis. The self-renewing model has atrophied into second-hand memory and dogma, a dogma that the fearful, the uninformed, and the emotionally troubled feel a need to defend with violent action.

The potential for violence is especially high when humanity stands, as it does today, at a crossroads of myth and religio-political fanaticism. In twelve years we'll enter a new millennium. On the millennial threshold, hordes of overly susceptible people tend to become swept up in feverish visions of "the end of the world." The desire for a fresh start, for an end to worry, work, and personal responsibility, mixes with mad prophecy and with what author Eleanor Munro has called "faith in the Pilgrim Lord's millennial return," to produce volatile psychological anticipation.

In the past, humankind on the whole has successfully weathered those storms, but whenever a segment has failed to comprehend the essentially symbolic nature of apocalypse (as in Judea at the waning of the last millennium BC), genocide has resulted. Prophecy self-fulfilled. Munro asks the chilling question, "How far does this myth still affect political destiny, by implanting structures in the minds of millions that must be fulfilled in historic time?"

In other words, if we expect and/or secretly covet Doomsday, we can make it happen. Those strange bedfellows, the rigid ignoramuses of the religious right and the comet-chasing, earthquake-fancying, harmonic-convergence-befuddled innocents of the New Age, share a misinterpretation of eschatological legend that is downright scary in intensity and scope. In its passionate if misguided longing to transcend the disorderliness, friction, and unpredictability that characterize life, it strikes me as a death wish on a global scale – but one that could be reversed with a basic understanding of mythology.

The Moyers–Campbell series does not deal with the millennialism issue in any direct way, don't let me mislead you, but by simply reintroducing us to the mythic underpinnings of our culture and consciousness, it can help yank us from the jaws of the dragon and set us down once more in the magnificent labyrinth whose twists and turns it is our sacred privilege to go on negotiating for millennia still to come.

In *Joseph Campbell and the Power of Myth,* you will hear

extraordinary stories told by a master storyteller, and you will see temples, art objects, and ceremonies you may have never seen before, as well as the antics of familiar heroes and heroines: astronauts, artists, actors, and athletes. Which is to say, the programs are entertaining as well as edifying.

They do tend to be visually static at times. It's the nature of the medium. And while Moyers and Campbell play off one another fairly well, they're not Wally Shawn and André Gregory. Nevertheless, there're moments when Moyers, resembling a puckish George Bush, does seem to be having his mind blown during a scene from *My Dinner With Joe*. As interviews go, these are more conversational, less confrontational than many, but a subtly crisp dynamic does emerge.

What does not quite emerge is Campbell's true personality. Oh, we get his twinkle, his halting eloquence, his robust but ever courtly assertiveness (a former world-class runner, he provides all aspiring octogenarians with an image to shoot for), but his private dimensions are left draped in opaque silks.

Well, so what? Perhaps we don't need to know that Campbell was a dignified neo-Victorian gentleman, minus any trace of the sexual hang-ups associated with the type. Or that for the last forty years of his life he refused to read a newspaper and did not attend a motion picture until the day before his eightieth birthday when he sat through the entire *Star Wars* trilogy, one picture after the other. Or that socially he was barely to the left of William F. Buckley, harboring a withering contempt for the clamorings and phobias of the mindless masses. (Upon our return from Mexico, he vowed he'd never again set foot South of the Border: it was just too funky for him, too awash in lurid emotions.) He could appear haughty at times, but at his age and with his knowledge and accomplishments, he may be excused for not suffering fools gladly.

(And speaking of fools, you may have heard that there are thought police from our academic left who would tar the myth master with the anti-Semitic brush. This is hogwash. Far from attacking Jews, Campbell, an honest, uncompromising scholar, simply made the observation – non-arbitrarily and in proper context – that the ancient Hebrews failed to establish a high culture as did, for example, the Greeks, Egyptians, Chinese, Romans, Aztec, Inca, et al.; a nomadic people, they produced no great art, architecture, science, or centers of learning. What the Hebrews did do was engender, embellish, codify, and amplify Levantine legend, legend that still impacts the modern world, legend that Campbell spent a lifetime interpreting, if not always to the satisfaction of the sanctimonious.)

Despite his disappointment in contemporary humanity, however, Campbell maintained an enormous, contagious enthusiasm for what he called "the rapture of being alive." That enthusiasm flares in the PBS series like a bonfire in a Druid glade. In fact, Campbell insisted that the Moyers interviews were not about meaning but experience, an experience of life in its whole geometric array of facets and phases.

So you watch this enlightening series, beginning to end. And after the final episode, you turn off your TV set. Moments later, a woodsman's ax with blue eyes and a mossy handle flies in your bedroom window. Don't be alarmed. True, it may want to marry you. On the other hand, it may have dropped by to invite you to the coronation of the Ant King. Accept, in either case. After all, as Joseph Campbell was fond of pointing out, "The myth is *you*."

Seattle Weekly, 1988

Nadja Salerno-Sonnenberg

Play for us, you big wild gypsy girl, you who look as if you might have spent the morning digging potatoes on the steppes of Russia; you who surely galloped in on a snorting mare, bareback or standing in the saddle; you whose chicory tresses reek of bonfire and jasmine; you who traded a dagger for a bow: grab your violin as if it were a stolen chicken, roll your perpetually startled eyes at it, scold it with that split beet dumpling you call a mouth; fidget, fuss, flounce, flick, fume – and fiddle: fiddle us through the roof, fiddle us over the moon, higher than rock 'n' roll can fly; saw those strings as if they were the log of the century, fill the hall with the ozone of your passion; play Mendelssohn for us, play Brahms and Bruch; get them drunk, dance with them, wound them, and then nurse their wounds, like the eternal female that you are; play until the cherries burst in the orchard, play until wolves chase their tails in the tearooms; play until we forget how we long to tumble with you in the flower beds under Chekhov's window; play, you big wild gypsy girl, until beauty and wildness and longing are one.

Esquire, 1989

The Genius Waitress

Of the genius waitress, I now sing.

Of hidden knowledge, buried ambition, and secret sonnets scribbled on cocktail napkins; of aching arches, ranting cooks, condescending patrons, and eyes diverted from ancient Greece to ancient grease; of burns and pinches and savvy and spunk; of a uniquely American woman living a uniquely American compromise, I sing. I sing of the genius waitress.

Okay, okay, she's probably not really a genius. But she *is* well-educated. She has a degree in Sanskrit, ethnoastronomy, Icelandic musicology, or something equally valued in the contemporary marketplace. Even if she could find work in her chosen field, it wouldn't pay beans – so she slings them instead. (The genius waitress is not to be confused with the aspiring-actress waitress, so prevalent in Manhattan and Los Angeles and so different from her sister in temperament and I.Q.)

As a type, the genius waitress is sweet and sassy, funny and smart; young, underestimated, fatalistic, weary, cheery (not happy, cheerful: there's a difference and she understands it), a tad bohemian, often borderline alcoholic, frequently pretty (though her hair reeks of kitchen and bar); as independent as a cave bear (though ever hopeful of "true love") and, above all, *genuine*.

Covertly sentimental, she fusses over toddlers and old folks, yet only fear of unemployment prevents her from handing an obnoxious customer his testicles with his bill.

She doesn't mind a little good-natured flirting, and if you flirt with verve and wit, she may flirt back. Never, however, *never* try to impress her with your résumé. Her tolerance for pretentious Yuppies ends with her shift, sometimes earlier. She reads men like a menu and always knows when she's being offered leftovers or an artificially inflated soufflé.

Should you ever be lucky enough to be taken home by her to that studio apartment with the jerry-built bookshelves and Frida Kahlo posters, you will discover that whereas in the public dining room she is merely as proficient as she needs to be, in the private bedroom she is blue gourmet virtuoso. Five stars and counting! Afterward, you can discuss chaos theory or the triple aspects of the mother goddess in universal art forms – while you massage her swollen feet.

Eventually, she leaves food service for graduate school or marriage, but unless she wins a grant or a fair divorce settlement, chances are she'll be back, a few years down the line, reciting the daily specials with her own special mixture of warmth and ennui.

Erudite emissary of eggs over easy, polymath purveyor of polenta and prawns, articulate angel of apple pie, the genius waitress is on duty right now in hundreds of U.S. restaurants, smile at the ready, sauce on the side. So brush up on your Schopenhauer, place your order – and tip, mister, tip. She deserves a break today.

Of her, I sing.

Playboy, 1991

Ray Kroc

If cows watched horror movies, everybody knows who their favorite monster would be.

Imagine that it's Friday midnight down on the farm and the Guernseys and the Angus are gathered around the barnyard TV, spellbound by the rerun of that classic bovine chiller, *Teats Up,* when suddenly the lights flicker, organ music swells, and onto the screen ambles a chesty, cherubic octogenarian in a business suit, swinging a cleaver and flashing a mystic ring with symbolic golden arches on it, and, oh, a terrified moo rises from the herd and there is much trembling of udder and tail. At that moment, a little bullock in the back is heard to ask, "Mommy, on Halloween can I go as Ray Kroc?"

To cattle, Ray Kroc is the franchise Frankenstein, the Hitler behind a Hereford holocaust, a fiend who has sent about 550,000 of their relatives to the grinder, grinning all the while and encouraging his henchmen with his macabre credo, "Remember, ten patties to the pound!"

It's scant comfort to the cows that Kroc has also doomed fifty million cucumbers to be pickled and chopped, or that he's boiled more than half a billion potatoes in oil. Apparently, potatoes and cukes don't mind. They're said to like being processed. It's their idea of emancipation.

Botanists, especially if they're Catholic, might argue that

since cucumbers are, in fact, the ovaries of the cucumber plant, they can be fulfilled only through reproduction, but the truth is, many such vegetables are sick and tired of being regarded as sex objects and baby factories; they want to break out of the mold, to travel and meet people and be appreciated for themselves, and Kroc gives them that opportunity. If pickles wore sandals, Ray Kroc would be Moses. But that's another story.

Whether one chooses to mourn with the meats or rejoice with the veggies is a religious decision and nobody's business but one's own. The point here is not that Kroc has wiped out considerable fauna and flora, nor that he's become thunderously wealthy in the process, but that the manner in which he merchandises his victims' remains has transformed the United States of America.

Kroc, of course, is the man behind McDonald's. He was a middle-aged milkshake-machine salesman out of Chicago when, in 1954, he called on an account in San Bernardino and saw the future. Its name was fast foods.

Curious about how a little California drive-in could keep eight of his Multi-mixers running continuously, Kroc found a restaurant stripped down to the minimum in service and menu, a precision shop turning out fries, beverages, and fifteen-cent hamburgers on an assembly line. The brainchild of the McDonald boys, Mac and Dick, it combined speed, simplicity, and edibility to a degree that made Kroc giddy, especially when the brothers readily agreed to sell him the rights for national development. It was as if Henry Ford had married Mom's Apple Pie and adopted Ray as their son and heir.

Mac and Dick McDonald, never overly ambitious, were more of a hindrance than a help, but Kroc, an energetic dreamer, built a $7.8 billion empire of 7,400 drive-ins and somewhere along the way named the Big Mac double burger after one of the brothers. (Since these are "family" restaurants, it's easy to understand why it wasn't named for the other one.)

Modern America is dominated – environmentally, cultur-ally, and psychologically – by freeways, and it has been McDonald's and its imitators (Go Burger King! Go Wendy's! Go Jack in the Box!) that have nurtured our freeway con-sciousness and allowed it to bloom. In the past, hungry motorists could look through their windshields and pick and choose from a glorious ongoing lineup of diners, truck stops, and barbecue pits, but such an array of roadside attractions would defeat the purpose of a freeway, as would the time and trouble involved if a driver had to exit at random and search an unfamiliar neighborhood for the unfamiliar restaurant that might suit his or her schedule, pocketbook, and taste.

Thanks to Kroc, the migrating masses simply aim their pro-truding stomachs at the landmark arches, sinuous of form and sunny of hue, and by the first belch they're back on the road, fast fed and very nearly serene, which is to say, no cashier has cheated them; no maître d' has insulted them; no tempera-mental chef, attractive waitress, or intriguing flavor has delayed them; they've neither gagged on a greasy spoon nor tripped over an *x* in a *oie roti aux pruneaux*. With McDonald's, they're secure.

That's the fly in the Egg McMuffin. Rather, the fly is that there never *is* a fly in an Egg McMuffin. The human spirit requires surprise, variety, and risk in order to enlarge itself. Imagination feeds on novelty. As imagination emaciates, options diminish; the fewer our options, the more bleak our prospects and the greater our susceptibility to controls. The wedding of high technology and food service has produced a robot cuisine, a totalitarian burger, the standardized sustenance of a Brave New World.

McDonald's not only cooks with computers, assuring that every tiny French fry is identical in color, texture, and temper-ature, but its "specially designed dispensers" see to it that the

Big Mac you may scarf today in Seattle has exactly the same amount of "special sauces" on it as the one your cousin gobbled last month near Detroit. If that extreme of uniformity doesn't ring your alarm, you've already half-moved into the B. F. Skinner anthill.

And yet . . . We still live in a pluralistic society, where there are probably more than enough French-cooking classes and Mexican fusion sushi bars to satisfy the educated palate and the adventurous tongue. Moreover, "gourmet" burger chains, such as the Red Robin and Hamburger Hamlet, are on the rise.

So what if democracy tends to sanctify mediocrity and McDonald's represents mediocrity at its zenith, its most sublime? Fast foods are perfectly suited for America, for a population on the move; a fluid, informal people, unburdened by a pretension or tradition; a sweetly vulgar race, undermined by its own brash naïveté rather than by Asian stoicism or European angst. Today there are McDonald's in Tokyo and Vienna, but they don't blend in and never will. Here, they are at the heart of the matter, reductive kitchens for a classless culture that hasn't time to dally on its way to the next rainbow's end.

When there are dreams to be chased, greener pastures to be grazed, deadlines to be met, tests to be taken, malls to be shopped, Little Leaguers to be feted, sitcoms to be watched, or lonely apartments to be avoided, we refuel in flight. Hookups such as McDonald's make it easy, if banal.

Columbus discovered America, Jefferson invented it, Lincoln unified it, Goldwyn mythologized it, and Kroc Big Mac'd it. It could have been an omniscient computer that provided this land with its prevailing ambiance, it might have been an irresistible new weapons system, a political revolution, an art movement, or some gene-altering drug. Isn't it just a little bit wonderful that it was a hamburger?

For a hamburger is warm and fragrant and juicy. A hamburger is soft and non-threatening. It personifies the Great Mother herself, who has nourished us from the beginning.

A hamburger is an icon of layered circles, the circle being at once the most spiritual and most sensual of shapes. A hamburger is companionable and faintly erotic: the nipple of the Goddess, the bountiful belly-ball of Eve. You are what you think you eat.

Best of all, a hamburger doesn't take itself seriously. Thus, it embodies that generous sense of humor that persists in America even as our bacon burns and our cookies crumble. McDonald's has served forty-five billion burgers, and every single one of them has had a smile on its face.

So, to Ray Kroc grant a pardon for his crimes against cows, stay his sentence for having ambushed our individuality at Standardization Gulch, order him to perform no more than, say, fifty thousand hours of community service for turning us into a waddling race of lard-assed chubs. Yes, he has changed our habits, undeniably for the worse, but a man who can say of himself, as Kroc did, that "it requires a certain kind of mind to see beauty in a hamburger bun" is a man who can cut the mustard.

Esquire, 1983

Jennifer Jason Leigh

I want to tell you about the Lizard Queen, I want to tell you about the Shape Changer, I want to tell you about a cuter chimera and a darker rose, I want to tell you about the triple aspects of the Universal Goddess – maiden, mother, and crone; or waif, whore, and witch – as manifest in a single petite young actress from Southern California, whose name you might recognize yet whose looks you would be hard put to describe because she is so dramatically different from movie to movie that you would swear she is not one woman but an encyclopedia of women, a feminine panoply: the three thousand faces of Eve.

I want to tell you that she is a truth-seeking missile, that when developing a role she goes directly for the character's soul and then fills in around it with disturbingly accurate minutiae. Her triumph is her willingness to descend into the green ooze at the bottom of the psyche, down among the rats and black beetles, only to emerge clutching something gracious, something good, some stained and dented emotional equivalent of the Holy Grail.

And I ought to tell you that while she may be quietly incandescent on both the screen and the set, should you encounter her between films you would find her unassumedly running the most humdrum of daily errands and greeting your questions about her art with a giggle so musical and shy that Marilyn Monroe could have gargled with it. A lack of pretension enhances her power to pretend.

Finally, regarding her paradoxical persona – fly and spider, sunbeam and twister, custard spoon and skinning knife – allow me to report that Alan Rudolph, who directed her marrow-piercing performance in *Mrs. Parker and the Vicious Circle*, once said, "When I first met her, I wanted to protect her. After I got to know her, I wanted her to protect me."

Her name is Jennifer Jason Leigh. Let's take her little hand in ours. Then let's ask her to guard us, too, against the brutal shadows that she, with incongruous innocence, seems to understand so well.

Esquire, 1994

Leonard Cohen

He was rowed down from the north in a leather skiff manned by a crew of trolls. His fur cape was caked with candle wax, his frown stained blue by wine – though the latter was seldom noticed due to the fox mask he wore at all times. A quill in his teeth, a solitary teardrop a-squirm in his palm, he was the young poet prince of Montreal, handsome, immaculate, searching for sturdier doors to nail his poignant verses on.

In Manhattan, grit drifted into his ink bottle. In Vienna, his spice box exploded. On the Greek isle of Hydra, Orpheus came to him at dawn astride a transparent donkey and restrung his cheap guitar. From that moment on, he shamelessly and willingly exposed himself to the contagion of music. To the furtive religio-sexual inquisitiveness of the solemn seeker was added the openly foolhardy passion of the romantic troubadour. By the time he returned to America, songs were working in him like bees in an attic and connoisseurs were developing cravings for his nocturnal honey, despite the fact that hearts were occasionally stung.

Now, thirty years later, as society staggers toward the millennium, flailing and screeching all the while, like an orangutan with a steak knife in its side, Leonard Cohen – his vision, his gift, his perseverance – is finally getting his due. It may be because he speaks to this wounded zeitgeist with particular eloquence and accuracy, it may be merely cultural time-lag, yet another example of the slow-to-catch-on many opening their ears belatedly to what the few have been hearing all along. In any case, the glitter curtain has shredded, the boogie-woogie gate has rocked loose from its hinges, and here sits L. Cohen at an altar in the garden, staidly enjoying newfound popularity and expanded respect.

From the beginning, his musical peers have recognized Cohen's ability to establish succinct analogies among life's realities, his talent for creating intimate relationships between the interior world of longing and language and the exterior world of trains and violins. Even those performers who have neither "covered" his compositions nor been overtly influenced by them have professed to admire their artfulness: the darkly delicious melodies – aural bouquets of gardenia and thistle – that bring to mind an electrified, de-Germanized Kurt Weill; the playfully (and therefore dangerously) mournful lyrics that can peel the apple of love and the peach of lust with a knife that cuts all the way to the mystery, a layer Cole Porter just couldn't expose.

It is their desire to honor L. Cohen, songwriter, that has prompted a delegation of our brightest artists to climb, one by one, joss sticks smoldering, the steep and salty staircase in the Tower of Song.

There is evidence that the honoree might be privy to the secret of the universe, which, in case you're wondering, is simply this: everything is connected. *Everything.* Many, if not most, of the links are difficult to determine. The instrument, the apparatus, the focused ray that can uncover and illuminate those connections is language. And just as a sudden infatuation often will light up a person's biochemical sky more pyrotechnically than any deep, abiding attachment, so an unlikely, unexpected burst of linguistic imagination will usually reveal greater truths than the most exacting scholarship. In fact, the poetic image may be the only device remotely capable of dissecting romantic desire, let alone disclosing the hidden mystical essence of the material world.

Cohen is a master of the quasi-surrealistic phrase, of the "illogical" line that speaks so directly to the unconscious that surface ambiguity is transformed into ultimate, if fleeting, comprehension: comprehension of the bewitching nuances of sex and the bewildering assaults of culture. Undoubtedly, it is to his lyrical mastery that his prestigious colleagues now pay tribute. Yet, there may be something else. As various, as distinct, as rewarding as each of their expressions are, there can still be heard in their individual interpretations the distant echo of Cohen's own voice, for it is his singing voice as well as his writing pen that has breathed life into these songs.

It is a voice raked by the claws of Cupid, a voice rubbed raw by the philosopher's stone. A voice marinated in kirschwasser, sulfur, deer musk, and snow; bandaged with sackcloth from a ruined monastery; warmed by the embers left down near the river after the gypsies have gone.

It is a penitent's voice, a rabbinical voice, a crust of unleavened vocal toast – spread with smoke and subversive wit. He has a voice like a carpet in an old hotel, like a bad itch on the hunchback of love. It is a voice meant for pronouncing the names of women – and cataloging their sometimes hazardous charms. Nobody can say the word "naked" as nakedly as Cohen. He makes us see the markings where the pantyhose have been.

Finally, the actual everyday persona of their creator may be said to haunt these songs, although details of his private lifestyle can be only surmised. A decade ago, a teacher who called himself Shree Bhagwan Rajneesh came up with the name "Zorba the Buddha" to describe the ideal modern man: a contemplative man who maintains a strict devotional bond with cosmic energies, yet is completely at home in the physical realm. Such a man knows the value of the dharma and the value of the Deutschemark, knows how much to tip a waiter in a Paris nightclub and how many times to bow in a Kyoto shrine; a man who can do business when business is necessary, yet allow his mind to enter a pine cone or his feet to dance in wild abandon if moved by the tune. Refusing to turn his back on beauty, this Zorba the Buddha character finds in sensual pleasures not a contradiction but an affirmation of the spiritual self. Doesn't he sound a lot like Leonard Cohen?

We have been led to picture Cohen spending his mornings meditating in Armani suits, his afternoons wrestling the muse, his evenings sitting in cafés where he eats, drinks, and speaks soulfully but seductively with the pretty larks of the street. Quite possibly this is a distorted portrait. The apocryphal, however, has a special kind of truth.

It doesn't really matter. What matters here is that after thirty years, L. Cohen is holding court in the lobby of the whirlwind, and that giants have gathered to pay him homage. To him – and to us – they bring the offerings they have hammered from his iron, his lead, his kryptonite, his sexual nitrogen, his gold.

Tower of Song, 30-year tribute album, liner notes, 1995

Slipper Sipping

With the exception of chocolate dentures, there's probably nothing in this world more impractical than glass shoes: their life expectancy must be as short as their discomfort level is horrific. So, was Cinderella a naïve ditz, a dingbat with masochistic tendencies? Did her fairy godmother, who presumably possessed the power to conjure up the finest Milanese leathers, have a twisted sense of humor? Or was there some hidden logic behind sending the humble little hearth honey to the royal ball shod in brittle silica?

Surely, the last. Fairy Godmother's intention obviously was to try to entice Prince Charming (alas, not the sharpest knife in the drawer) to sip champagne from one of Cinderella's slippers.

Why? Because no gesture in the annals of romantic behavior is quite as auspicious as drinking a toast from a woman's footwear. Any dull swain can buy a girl flowers, candy, or even a ring, treat her to a movie or a weekend at a spa, but a man who'll quaff from a shoe-in-use is a man who, in the name of love, will stop at almost nothing. The woman so honored may be absolutely confident that this date-night daredevil is not among the faint of heart. If only at floor level, he is committed. Better yet, the dude is fun!

Walking as it does a thin line between exhibitionism and

intimacy, between chivalry and perversity, the very act of the shoe-sip allows debonair zeal to vibrate ever so slightly with the distant thrill of kinkiness. Symbolism aside (see Freud on shoes), it flirts with danger, even should the risk involved be nothing greater than a stained insole. (A real sport will later blot the lining dry with a clean handkerchief or the tail of his shirt.)

Flavored, if only in the imagination, with the sweet pink of toe meat; barnacled with tar, bubblegum, or something much worse; a friend of the earth, survivor of tack and shard; tasseled tramp, buckle-bedecked blistermeister, grunt soldier bearing the muddied flag of fashion, sailor of the woven and grouted seas; streetwise, dance-dizzy, blind as an ol' blues cat, the lowly shoe – no matter how elegant or expensive, a slipper can never conceal its utilitarian roots or its kinship to beasts – the shoe must be shocked to suddenly find itself a vessel ferrying luxurious bubbles to a lover's lips. And its astonishment only mirrors the surprise of its owner, for no female, not even a Gabor or Lola Montez, is ever so jaded as to be prepared for, or unimpressed by, the man who impetuously and ceremoniously sates his thirst from her pump.

For all of its spontaneity, however, the impromptu shoe-swig does possess a certain protocol. While there may be something verbally poetic about slurping a Singapore sling from a slingback or chugging cappuccino from a Capezio, those variations, in practice, will never do. The chosen shoe may be any color or style – so long, of course, as it isn't open-toed or pathetically orthopedic – but the beverage consumed from it can be only champagne. No beer, no gin, milk, tea, Diet Coke, or bathwater; not even a fine cognac or vintage bordeaux. Champagne, and champagne alone, with its fizz of stardust, its gilded sparks, its secret singing and tiny bursts of light, only champagne has the magic to transform a shoe into a holy chalice, and the shoe-sup (on the surface of it, a rather silly piece of business) into a kind of wild kinetic sonnet, a pantomime of reckless adoration.

Because of the manner in which it combines playfulness with passion, the way that it both galvanizes the moment and anticipates the future, imbibing champagne from a suitable slipper may constitute the perfect salute to the new millennium.

When the little cobbled skiff of womanhood is swamped with Mumm's Extra Dry, when that pedestrian article that cushions the heel and supports the arch is invaded by the tongue, when devotion is enlivened by audacity, and longing refuses to limit itself to conventional expression, well, anything can happen. Anything.

What wiser way, then, to face the Big Tomorrow than with an open mind, an adventurous spirit, and a romantic heart; ready, even eager, for come-what-may? Fairy Godmother knew this. That's why she conjured up the wearable goblet. And why it got results.

So, pass those high heels, baby, and don't spare the stiletto. Here's looking at you – from the ground up. And Happy 21st Century!

Bergdorf Goodman, 1999

Redheads

Red hair is a woman's game.

The harsh truth is, most red-haired men look like blondes who've spoiled from lack of refrigeration. They look like brown-haired men who've been composted out behind the barn. Yet that same pigmentation that on a man can resemble leaf mold or junkyard rust, a woman wears like a tiara of rubies.

Not only are female redheads frequently lovely but theirs is a loveliness that suggests both lust and danger, pleasure and violence, and is, therefore, to the male of the species virtually irresistible. Red – Code Red – were the tresses of the original femme fatale.

Of course, much of the "fatale" associated with redheads is illusory, a stereotypical projection on the part of sexually neurotic men. Plenty of redheads are as demure as rosebuds and as sweet as strawberry pie. However, the mere fact that they are *perceived* to be stormy, if not malicious, grants them a certain license and a certain power. It's as if bitchiness is their birthright. By virtue of their coloration, they possess a congenital permit to be terrible and lascivious, which, even if never exercised, sets them apart from the remainder of womankind, who have traditionally been expected to be mild and pure.

Now that women are demolishing those old misogynistic expectations, will redheads lose their special magic, will Pippi Longstocking come to be regarded as just one of the girls: Heidi with a fever, Snow White at the beach? Hardly. To believe that blondes and brunettes are simply redheads in repressive drag is to believe that UFOs are kiddie balloons. All redheads, you see, are mutants.

Whether they spring from genes disarranged by earthly forces or are "planted" here by overlords from outer space is a matter for scholarly debate. It's enough for us to recognize that redheads are abnormal beings, bioelectrically connected to realms of strange power, rage, risk, and ecstasy.

What is your mission among us, you daughters of ancient Henna, you agents of the harvest moon? Are those star maps that your freckles replicate? How do you explain the fact that you live longer than the average human? Where did you get such sensitive skin? And why are your curls the same shade as heartache?

Alas, inquiry is futile: either they don't know or they won't say – and who has the nerve to pressure a redhead? We may never learn their origin or meaning, but it probably doesn't matter. We will go on leaping out of our frying pans into their fire, grateful for the opportunity to be titillated by their vengeful fury, real or imagined, and to occasionally test our erotic mettle in the legendary inferno of their passion.

Redheaded women! Those blood oranges! Those cherry bombs! Those celestial shrews and queens of copper! May they never cease to stain our white-bread lives with supernatural catsup.

GQ, 1988

Alan Rudolph

In the smart and lively movies of Alan Rudolph, nuances are at work like bees in a hive. A busy swarm of subtleties generates a nucleus of narrative honeycomb that has more layers than an archeologist's wedding cake, and the energized reticulum is all the more amazing because its intricacies seem at first ambiguous and offhand.

Horizontal layers of lust and angst crisscross with vertical layers of wit and beauty (despite modest budgets, every Rudolph film is delicious to the eye and ear), but the layer that most delights me (and drives the dullards daft) is the oblique stratum of goofiness that angles through his cinematic matrix like a butter knife that forgot to take its lithium and turned into a corkscrew.

For many people, "goofy" might suggest a kind of good-natured stupidity. With humorous overtones. Practiced observation, however, has led me to define goofiness as "user-friendly weirdness." With humorous overtones. And that is the definition intended here.

In case anybody has failed to notice, our little planet is *très* bizarre. Some of our weirdness is violent and horrific, ranging from fully flowered genocidal warfare to the secret buds of personal evil that David Lynch likes to press in his small-town scrapbooks. Far more prevalent – yet decidedly more difficult for a serious artist to capture – is the non-threatening variety of weirdness; the weirdness of the quirk, the tic, the discrepancy, the idiosyncrasy half-concealed, the passionate impulse that when indulged puts a strange new spin on the heart.

All of our lives are at least a trifle haywire, particularly in the area of romantic relationships. It is Rudolph's special genius to illuminate those haywire tendencies and reveal how they – and not convention or rationality – channel the undermost currents of our being. It is precisely Rudolph's attention to our so-called "off-the-wall" behavior that gives pictures such as *Choose Me, The Moderns,* and *Trouble in Mind* their comic and erotic freshness, their psychological veracity, their ovoid contours.

"Ovoid" is the correct description, although "elliptical" will do. Football-shaped at any rate. Most films or novels or plays bounce like basketballs, which is to say, up and down, up and down, traveling in a forward direction in a generally straight line. Rudolph's movies, on the other hand, bounce like footballs: end over end, elusively, changing direction, even reversing direction; wobbly, unpredictable, and wild. Goofy, in other words, like so much of life itself. Most of his films produce the aesthetic, emotional, and intellectual equivalents of gridiron kickoffs, followed by bone-cracking tackles or exhilarating returns.

When considering Alan Rudolph, it is crucial not to overlook those jarring hits. As charming and tinged with fantasy as his work can be, it is not fueled by froth. Even a walleyed strut such as *Songwriter* has its dark, serrated edges; and when they cut, they cut deep. The director possesses an urban sensibility, which he focuses sardonically on the sorrows as well as the pleasures of metropolitan romance. Who could sit through *Afterglow,* for example, without feeling that they'd been both whipsawed and lovingly massaged.

The miracle of Rudolph is how he manages to be gritty and

dreamy at the same time, even somber and funny at the same time. Not funny in one scene, somber in the next, but funny and somber *simultaneously*. This is a form of profundity that only the nimble-minded can totally appreciate, which eliminates . . . well, you know who it eliminates. I suspect it is the virtuoso manner with which he orchestrates nuances that allows him to ply the tragicomic paradox so successfully.

In any case, those almost surreal interpenetrations of melancholia and gaiety amplify the sense of mystery that haunts Rudolph's every movie if not his every scene (many of which unfold in smoky, neon-lit clubs and bars). What is present here is neither the prosaic mystery of whodunit nor the sentimental mystery of will-boy-get-girl – each a formulaic device calculated to manipulate an audience by means of manufactured suspense – but rather that transcendental mystery that swirls around our innermost longings and that can liberate an audience by connecting it viscerally to the greater mystery of existence.

In the marvelous *Love at Large,* Rudolph (who usually writes his own scripts) has Anne Archer ask Tom Berenger if they will be "glad and dizzy all the time." Ultimately, no matter how moody or bittersweet a Rudolph movie might be, when I walk out of the theater I feel somehow glad and dizzy. If you are aware of a better way to feel, please phone me right now. Collect.

Writers on Directors, Watson-Guptill, 1999

Miniskirt Feminism

Even though as a novelist and as a person I have long since left the period behind me, I remain convinced that the years 1964–72 were spiritually and politically the most momentous our nation has ever known, a time (destined to be endlessly maligned and misunderstood) when actual transcendence was in the air, and the words "land of the free and the home of the brave" began to be taken literally by some Americans, much to the chagrin of others.

Yet, considering all the ferment, foment, experimentation, and illumination that characterized the era, I must say it had some surprising aesthetic deficiencies, particularly in the realm of furnishings and décor.

While the myriad thrift-shop tapestries, Persian carpets, overstuffed sofas, beaded lampshades, peacock feathers, incense burners, macramé wall hangings, paisley cushions, and florid neo-Nouveau poster art provided a soft, tactile, sensually rich environment in which to get congenially, entertainingly, and even enlighteningly stoned, there was something about it – the clutter, the closeness, the inevitable moth-eaten dustiness and fake Orientalism of it – that was as cloying as the parlor of a Victorian vicar.

Whether I inhaled or not, it made me want to cough.

The rooms I chose to inhabit back then are very much like

the ones I dwell in now: interiors in which an array of clean, bold, simple, primary colors are set against a background of starkest white. My décor guru has always been Matisse, to whom I've instinctively turned in matters of taste, shunning the busy business of Klimt, Beardsley, and Jerry Garcia. Having said that, however, I can think of two material items from the 60s that ought to be honored: the miniskirt for its glorious debut, the brassiere for the martyrdom it suffered in exile.

The widespread donning of the miniskirt and doffing of the bra symbolized a burbling rebellion against constraint – sexual, societal, political, and religious. Among other things, our culture was being refeminized, and unharnessed women in abbreviated loin-wrappings – looking good, feeling free! – expressed this in a way every bit as direct and immediate as men in frilly collars and waist-length hair. Old boundary lines were blurring like wet mascara, and much of the land was giddy with the hashish of social change. Humans, hopes, hemlines: all were as high as kites.

It wasn't merely that miniskirts (and their sisters in emancipated style, hot pants) were sexy. Rather, they were sexy in a decidedly playful way, a playfulness which carried over into many other aspects of life.

People were being playful in the face of adversity, violence, and turmoil. That's the sort of playfulness that can transcend whimsy and frivolity to become a form of wisdom, a means of survival, a kind of grace. Women might protest an unjust war or battle for civil rights, but as evidenced by their attire, they refused to let the issues of the day make victims of them or drag them down into dowdy despair.

Eventually, of course, the pendulum swung. On the one hand, the old Judeo-Christian fear of license precipitated a vicious backlash. On the other, when the mainstream press finally got around to embracing thigh-flash and bra smoke as definitive of and essential to the "with-it" modern woman, the spirit of mischief and revolt was compromised and all the fun expired. The party was over. Brassieres rose from the ashes and resumed their erstwhile duties. It was the miniskirt's turn to be burned.

Short-short skirts have come back several times since then. But you know I'm right when I say it's not the same. Indeed, it may no longer be possible to stitch a zeitgeist into a few square inches of cloth.

Ah, but while it lasted, the 60s miniskirt was a sight to behold. More than a garment, it was a flag without a country, a banner without a slogan, a pennant without a team. Leather or satin, snug or flared, smooth or pleated, sassy or coyly demure, it was the all-embracing banderole that flew from the masthead of a heroic escapade. It was the happy standard of the heart.

The New York Times, 1995

The Sixties

It must be really irritating to have come of age in the 1980s or 90s to find your decade – your very own historical moment – persistently overshadowed by The Decade That Will Not Die, the ten years that have stolen the show of the twentieth century and hogged the cultural limelight for as long as you can recall. Not only are the 1960s a hair (a long hair) in your generational soup, but if you're a thinking person you're aware of both the fallacy of decadism and how dangerous and dumb it can be to embalm yourself in the attractive amber of the past.

In most of our lives, for better or for worse, there occurs a period of peak experience, a time when we are at our best, when we meet some challenge, endure some ordeal, receive some special recognition, have some sustained, heretofore unimaginable fun, or just feel consistently happy and free. There's a tendency then to become psychologically frozen in that glad ice, turning ourselves into living fossils for the remainder of our existence.

For females, the retrograde flypaper is often summer camp or high school. For far too many American males, it has been the armed services; the one time in their lives when, relieved of parents, wives, children, dull routines, and responsibilities, their every need supported, they could enjoy camaraderie, travel, and adventure. An awful lot of America's leaders never outgrew their wartime exploits, and these old padnags – waving red-white-and-blue cattle prods and farting the low notes of the Star-Spangled Banner – have over and over again insisted on military solutions to economic disputes, a manifestation of arrested development for which the world has paid a hard and ugly price.

Gray-haired flower children, while infinitely more benign, can seem almost equally foolish. Yet it would be a mistake – a smug distortion – to dismiss the 60s as just an ordinary fucked-up decade with a good press agent. Not only did the 60s *differ* from the 50s, the 80s, the 90s, etc., they were in several significant ways *superior* to them; superior, for example, in the expenditure of both passion and compassion, superior in the number of romantic seekers and idealistic questers (bless them each and every one) searching for something more substantial than material success. From the perspective of the so-called counterculture (for a time, the "counterculture" functioned as the dominant culture), music was less superficial then, authority less respected, violence less tolerated, love less fettered, wealth less worshiped, power less coveted, guilt less shouldered, depression less indulged, and fear less shivered with. In the 60s, beauty had not yet been voted out of office by the art community, flirting hadn't been demonized as sexual harassment by the cops of correctness, and tickets to any number of nirvanas could be easily obtained at any number of outlets, ancient or futuristic, although as Hermann Hesse once cautioned us, "the Magic Theater is not for everyone."

Illumination, like it or not, is an elitist condition. In every era and in almost every area, there have resided tiny minorities of enlightened individuals living their lives just beyond the threshold, having prematurely breached the gateway to what conceivably could be humanity's next evolutionary phase, a phase whose actualization – if it's to come at all – is probably still many years down the line. In certain key periods of history, one or another of those elitist minorities has become sufficiently large and resonant to affect the culture as a whole.

Think of the age of Akhenaton in Egypt, the reign of Zoroaster in Persia, the golden ages of Greece and Islam, the several great periods of Chinese culture, and the European Renaissance. Something similar was brewing in America in the years 1964 to 1972.

Maybe it's sentimental, if not actually stupid, to romanticize the 60s as an embryonic golden age. Obviously, this fetal age of enlightenment aborted. Nevertheless, while they lasted, the 60s were extraordinary. Like the Arthurian years at Camelot, they constituted a breakthrough, a fleeting moment of glory, a time when a significant little chunk of earthlings briefly realized their moral potential and flirted with their neurological destiny; a collective spiritual awakening that flared brilliantly until the brutal and mediocre impulses of the species drew tight once again the thick curtains of meathead somnambulism.

There's something else: I think it need be established, firmly, flatly, and finally, that what we call the 60s would never have happened had it not been for the introduction of psychedelic drugs into the prevailing American paradigm.

Certainly, there would have been protests, boycotts, and demonstrations, but they would have been only a fraction of the magnitude of those that actually occurred; they would have been far less frequent, widespread, intense, colorful, or effective.

The political and societal juggernaut of the 60s rolled on wheels of music, and that music owed both its aesthetic and ethical impetus to psychedelics. Eyes and hearts were opened – frequently by way of the ears – to fresh perceptions and utopian possibilities.

It was a dizzy period of transcendence and awareness: transcendence of compromised and obsolete value systems, awareness of the enormity and richness of a previously unsuspected inner reality. Its zeitgeist, despite what you may have heard, was only secondarily political. As much as it's been emphasized by uncomprehending journalists, the political movements of the time (be they pacifist, feminist, environmental, or racial) were largely the result of fallout from a *spiritual* explosion.

Now, in 1996 the word "spiritual" is, unfortunately, highly suspect. Yet, the changes in consciousness and in conscience that characterized and energized the 60s were of a sort that could only be described as oceanic. And they were a direct outgrowth of drug-inspired mysticism.

Thus, I contend that to talk about the 60s today without talking about, say, psilocybin, marijuana, and LSD, as, except in derisive asides, the media has been doing ad infinitum, is to be guilty of the most dishonest sort of revisionism. Moreover, a panel on the 60s that ignores or downplays the contribution of psychedelics would be akin to a panel on eggs that ignores or downplays the contribution of hens.

In closing, let me confess that were I granted a single ride in a time machine, I would *not* choose to be beamed back to 1967. No, as indelibly as that year is branded in the tissue of my memory, as exhilarating as it sometimes is to evoke, I've been there, done that, and I'd probably elect to travel instead to Paris during *La Belle Époque;* or to fifteenth-century Japan, where I might hit the meditation mat, the mountain trails, the sake bars, and the brothels with my idol, Ikkyu Sojun. However, my refusal to cling to my formative years doesn't mean that I'll ever sit quietly while clueless hacks, tedious scoldmuffins, and secretly envious kids malign a period of our recent history that towered above all others in shining promise, regardless of the fractures that promise may have suffered when it eventually fell off the ladder.

Introductory remarks at a panel discussion, Northwest Book Fest, 1996. Point No Point, 1996

Diane Keaton

A female circus clown was appearing at a shopping mall recently when a small child in the audience suddenly climbed onto her lap and gazed at her painted face with rapturous recognition. The child's mother began to weep. "My little boy is autistic," she explained. "This is the first time he has ever let another human touch him."

That incident reminded me of the actress Diane Keaton, and not because she sometimes looks as if P. T. Barnum dresses her. In her state of goofy grace, you see, Keaton possesses a kind of reality denied to ordinary beings. A kachina, a wondernik, a jill-o'-lantern, she is such an incandescent link to otherness that we introverts emerge blinking from our hiding holes and beg to have those strange hands touch us.

If she's some kind of phosphorescent flake, some kooky angel circling the ethers in deep left field; whether she won the eccentricity competition in the Miss California pageant or was actually in Istanbul at the time, none of that matters to those of us who love her. Give us half a chance and we'd lick hot fudge from her fingers, spank her with a ballet slipper, read aloud to her the sacred moon poems of Kalahari bushmen. What's more, we *like* the way she dresses.

Fantasies of compatibility aside, however, the fact is, if sex appeal was two grains of rice, Diane Keaton could feed the

Chinese army. (No? When was the last time you watched *Looking for Mr. Goodbar*?)

Her allure is partly due to the manner in which she combines a saucy bohemian brilliance with an almost disabling vulnerability, partly due to the hormonal aura of baby fat (tender and juicy) that surrounds her even when she is mature and svelte. Mainly, though, it's because of her smile – a smile that could paint Liberace's ceiling, butter a blind man's waffles, and slush the accumulated frosts of Finland Station.

The bonus of this beauteous and beatific bozo is that the older she gets, the sexier she gets. By the time she's fifty, she may have to wear a squid mask for self-protection.

Esquire, 1987

Kissing

Kissing is our greatest invention. On the list of great inventions, it ranks higher than the Thermos bottle and the Airstream trailer; higher, even, than room service, possibly because the main reason room service was created was so that people could stay in bed and kiss without going hungry.

The mirror is a marvelous invention, as well, yet its genesis didn't require a truckload of imagination, the looking glass being merely an extension of pond surface, made portable and refined. Kissing, on the other hand, didn't imitate nature so much as it restructured it. Kissing molded the face into a brand-new shape, the pucker shape, and then, like some renegade scientist grafting plops of sea urchin onto halves of ripe pink plums, it found a way to fuse the puckers, to meld them and animate them, so that one pucker rubbing against another generates heat, moisture, and a luminous neuro-muscular friction. Thomas Edison, switch off your dim bulb and slink away!

Tradition informs us that kissing, as we know it, was invented by medieval knights for the utilitarian purpose of determining whether their wives had been tapping the mead barrel while the knights were away on Crusades. If history is accurate for once, the kiss began as an osculatory wire tap or oral snoop, a kind of alcoholic chastity belt, after the fact.

Form is not always faithful to function, however, and gradually, kissing for kissing's sake became popular in the courts, spreading (trickle-down ergonomics) to tradesmen, peasants, and serfs. And why not? Transcending class and financial status, completely democratic in its mysterious capacity to deliver cascading pangs of immediate physical and emotional pleasure, kissing proved inherently if irrationally *sweet*. It was as if that modicum of atavistic sweetness still remaining in civilized western man was funneled into kissing and kissing alone.

Kissing is the supreme achievement of the *western* world. Orientals, including those who tended the North American continent before the land developers arrived from Europe in the 16th century, rubbed noses, and millions still do. Yet, despite the golden cornucopia of their millennia – they gave us yoga and gunpowder, Buddha and pasta – they, their multitudes, their saints and sages, never produced a kiss. (Oh, sure, the *Rig Veda,* a four-thousand-year-old Hindu text, makes reference to kissing, but who knows the precise nature of the activity to which the Sanskrit word alludes? Modern Asians, of course, have taken up kissing much as they've taken up the fork, though so far, they haven't improved upon it as they usually do with those foreign things they adopt.)

Kissing is the flower of the *civilized* world. So-called primitives, savages, Pygmies, and cannibals have shown tenderness to one another in many tactile ways, but pucker against pucker has not been their style. Tropical Africans touched lips, you say? Quite right, many of them did, as did aboriginal peoples in other parts of the world. Ah, but although their lips may have touched, they did not linger. And let's admit it, the peck is not much more than a square wheel, sterile and slightly ominous. With what else did Judas betray the Big Guy but a peck: terse, spit-free, and tongueless?

Kissing is the glory of the *human* species. All animals copulate but only humans osculate. Parakeets rub beaks? Sure they do, but only little old ladies who murder schoolchildren with knitting needles to steal their lunch money so that they can buy fresh kidneys to feed overweight kitty cats would place bird billing in the realm of the true kiss. There are primatologists who claim that apes exchange oral affection, but from here, the sloppy smacks of chimps look pretty incidental: at best, they're probably just checking to see if their mates have been into the fermented bananas. No, arbitrary beast-to-beast snout nuzzling may give narrators of wildlife films an opportunity to plumb new depths of anthropomorphic cuteness, but on Aphrodite's radar screen, it makes not a blip.

Psychologists claim that talking to our pets is a socially acceptable excuse for talking to ourselves. That may cast a particularly narcissistic light on those of you who *kiss* your pets, but you shouldn't let it stop you. Smooch your bulldog if you're so inclined. Buss your sister, your uncle, your grandpa, and anybody's bouncing baby. No kiss is ever wasted, not even on the lottery ticket kissed for luck. Kiss trees. Favorite books. Bowling balls. Old Jews sometimes kiss their bread before eating it, and those are good kisses, too. They resonate in the ozone.

The best kisses, though, are those between lovers, because those are the consequential ones, the risky ones, the transformative ones, the ones that call the nymphs and satyrs back to life, the many-layered kisses that we dive into as into a fairy-tale frog pond or the murky gene pool of our origins.

The fact that we enjoy watching others kiss may be less a matter of voyeurism than some sort of homing instinct. In any case, it explains the popular appeal of Hollywood and Paris. Who can forget the elastic thread of saliva that for one brief but electrifying second connected Yvonne De Carlo to Dan Duryea in *Black Bart*? And didn't Joni Mitchell's line "in France they kiss on Main Street" inspire hundreds of the romantically susceptible to pack their breath mints and head for Orly?

A final thought: beware the man who considers kissing as nothing more than duty, a sop to the "weaker" sex, an annoyingly necessary component of foreplay. That man has penis plaque in his arteries and will collapse under the weight of intimacy. Send him off to the nearest golf course while those of us who are more evolved celebrate the unique graces of the kiss:

No other flesh like lip flesh! No meat like mouth meat! The musical clink of tooth against tooth! The wonderful curiosity of tongues!

Playboy, 1990

Shree Bhagwan Rajneesh

I'm no disciple of Shree Bhagwan Rajneesh. I am not a disciple of *any* guru. I am, in fact, not convinced that the Oriental guru system is particularly useful to the evolution of consciousness in the western world (although I'll be the first to admit that what is most "useful" is not always what is most important). The very notion of guruhood seems at odds with the aspirations of the passionate individualist that I profess to be, and I'd be only slightly more inclined to entrust my soul to some holy man, however pure, than to a political committee or a psychiatrist.

So, I am no sannyasin. Ah, but I recognize the emerald breeze when it rattles my shutters, and Bhagwan is like a hard, sweet wind, circling the planet, blowing the beanies off of rabbis and popes, scattering the lies on the desks of the bureaucrats, stampeding the jackasses in the stables of the powerful, lifting the skirts of the pathologically prudish, and tickling the spiritually dead back to life.

Typhoon Bhagwan is not whistling Dixie. He is not peddling snake oil. He won't sell you a mandala that will straighten your teeth or teach you a chant that will make you a millionaire. Although he definitely knows which side his bread is Buddha-ed on, he refuses to play by the rules of the spiritual marketplace, a refreshing attitude, in my opinion, and one that stations him in some pretty strong company.

Jesus had his parables, Buddha his sutras, Mohammed his fantasies of the Arabian night. Bhagwan has something more appropriate for a species crippled by greed, fear, ignorance, and superstition: he has cosmic comedy.

What Bhagwan is out to do, it seems to me, is pierce our disguises, shatter our illusions, cure our addictions, and demonstrate the self-limiting and often tragic folly of taking ourselves too seriously. His pathway to ecstasy twists through the topsy-turvy landscape of the Ego as Joke.

Of course, a lot of people don't get the punchline. (How many, for example, realized that Bhagwan's ridiculous fleet of Rolls-Royces was one of the greatest spoofs of consumerism ever staged?) But while the jokes may whiz far over their heads, the authorities intuitively sense something dangerous in Bhagwan's message. Why else would they have singled him out for the kind of malicious persecution they never would have directed at a banana republic dictator or a Mafia don? If Ronald Reagan had had his way, this gentle vegetarian would have been crucified on the White House lawn.

The danger they intuit is that in Bhagwan's words, as in the psychedelic drugs that they suppress with an equally hysterical bias, there is information that, if properly assimilated, can help to set men and women loose from their control. Nothing frightens the state – or its partner in crime, organized religion – so much as the prospect of an informed population thinking for itself and living free.

Freedom is a potent wine, however. Its imbibers can take a long while to adjust to its intoxications. Some, including many sannyasins, never adjust. Patriotic Americans pay gassy lip service to their liberty, but as they've demonstrated time and time again, they *can't handle* liberty. Whether more than a fistful of Bhagwan's emulators can handle it has yet to be determined. It likely will take something more eschatologically dramatic than the unorthodox wisdom of a compassionate guru to dislodge most modern earthlings, be they seekers or suckers, from our age's double helix of corruption and apathy, let alone to facilitate the human animal's eventual escape from the web of time.

Meanwhile, though, we yearn for sound advice, and Bhagwan's discourses ring a lot truer than most. He has the vision to see through the Big Mask, the guts to express that vision regardless of the consequences, and the love and humor to place it all in a warmly mischievous perspective. Moreover, here is one teacher who is honest enough, illuminated enough, *alive* enough to openly enjoy the physical world while simultaneously pointing out its ubiquitous traps and trickeries. Zorba the Buddha!

Predictably, the journalists who've investigated Bhagwan have each and every one been befuddled by his methods, his messages, and the delightful paradoxes that they see only as flaky contradictions. Even many of Rajneesh's followers end up being confused by him. Well, Jesus left numerous contemporaries, including fellow Jewish reformers and his own disciples, in a comparable state. It goes with the territory, which is why they say in Zen, "The master is always killed on the road." Frequently he's killed by those who profess to love him most.

When Rajneeshis misbehave, the media and the public blame Rajneesh. They can't understand that he doesn't control them, has, in fact, no intention of ever trying to control them. The very notion of hierarchical control is antithetical to his teachings.

When Bhagwan learns of vile and stupid things done in his name, he only shakes his head and says, "I know they're crazy, but they have to go through it." That degree of freedom, that depth of tolerance, is as incomprehensible to the liberal hipster as it is to the rigid square. And yet, as an outsider who's been moved, impressed, and entertained by the manner in which Bhagwan has put the *fun* back in *profundity*, I know it's a level of wisdom that we simply must attain if we're to climb out of the insufferable mess we most aggressive of primates, with our hunger for order and our thirst for power, have made of this splendid world.

Introduction to *Bhagwan: The Most Godless Yet the Most Godly of Men,* by Dr. George Meredith, 1987

NOTE: When Bhagwan was shown the preceding remarks, he laughed and said that he didn't believe in Oriental guru systems either. In fact, he disavowed any connection to guruhood, saying that the very notion of a guru-disciple relationship is an affront to human dignity. He explained that since his emphasis had always been on just being oneself, the act of refusing to be *anybody's* disciple is precisely what being a disciple of Bhagwan is all about. Bingo! I believe he was speaking truthfully and I love him for it. In complaining that others have misrepresented Bhagwan, I misrepresented him myself, and for that I apologize.

Incidentally, as the reader probably is aware, not long before Bhagwan was poisoned by government assassins, he changed his name to Osho. At the Poona ashram, the name change was embraced so thoroughly, so fervently, one would have thought "Bhagwan" had never existed. It was almost reminiscent of one of those old Soviet appellation purges. However, I believe that had he lived, he would have eventually changed his name again, the whole point being, in my opinion, to demonstrate the ultimate fallacy of identifying with and becoming attached to one's name; or, for that matter, any other self-defining labels, including occupational titles and ethno-geographic distinctions. Who knows, had he survived, Bhagwan/Osho might have become Wolfgang, Bubba, or World B. Free.

Ruby Montana

When you learn that her name is Ruby Montana, you figure right away she's a cowgirl. An urban cowgirl. Which is to say, a make-believe cowgirl. Real cowgirls, working cowgirls, have less romantic names, such as Pat Futters or Debbie Jean Strunk. Still, Ruby is so appropriately booted, vested, and bandannaed that you wonder if she mightn't at least be a weekend rodeo queen. Ah, but then, far from the lone prairie, she drives up in a lurid two-tone 1955 Oldsmobile, removes a French horn from its trunk, and enters her house – a pink house, a house the color of the sorest saddle sore Dale Evans ever sat upon – and you conclude that she must be something else.

Something else, indeed.

In actuality, Ruby Montana is a popular Seattle shop-keeper. She is also that city's sweetheart of fantasy. For Ruby's imagination isn't simply tied to the hitching post of the make-believe cowgirl; her whole existence is an exercise in make-believe. In the world she has made for herself – a world built of neoteny, nuttiness, nostalgia, and kitsch; a world in which the secret life of objects is not only recognized but allowed to interface dramatically with her own life – Ruby daily demonstrates that reality is a matter of perception and that dreams don't come true, dreams are true.

Her shop, Ruby Montana's Pinto Pony, sells collectibles, and she herself is a collector. Should you follow her into that pink bungalow (its façade a hue similar to the Pepto-Bismol a nervous Daisy Lou chugs before the big barrel race), you would be amazed by both the extent of her collections and the artistry with which they are displayed. Every room is teeming: cookie jars, candlesticks, lamps (lava, figurative, and magic spinning), wall fish, ice buckets, ashtrays, bookends, German mythological prints, ranch furniture, Pee-wee Hermanesque gewgaws, Hollywood dime store Wild West memorabilia, and – in the Flamingo Room, the den where Ruby hopes to be sitting "when they drop the bomb" – a bar in the shape of a late 40s speedboat, aloha pillows, South Sea coffee tables, a shrine to Elvis, and twinkling tiki party lights. Inexplicably, all this sub-lowbrow ornamentation is arranged in a manner that approximates good, if freewheeling, taste. Roll partially over, Beethoven.

And we haven't even mentioned the salt and pepper shakers. Not that they could be overlooked, God no! There are hundreds of salt and peppers. Hundreds. Most of them unusual, many of them rare. They dominate the house. In some ways they dominate the owner of the house. They hold her much as a director is held by the various competing egos in his troupe. You see, Ruby Montana interacts with her treasures. She's involved with them. Dissatisfied with mere ownership, she doesn't accumulate knickknacks ("I despise that word!") to impress others or decorate a space. Ruby selects her salt and peppers carefully, and those that pass audition she plays with. She makes up tales about them. She casts them in private productions staged on Formica tabletops and kitchen shelves.

For example, there is the gay donkey (maybe salt, maybe pepper) whose parents can't handle his proclivities. Today, the donkey is dancing with his lover while Mom and Dad look on in bewilderment. There ensues poignant dialogue in which the hee-haw homosexual explains he's leaving town. So is the pig family next door, though the pigs, more happily, are off to Florida to attend a space launch: the dinnerware rocket is poised on its pad, presided over by JFK, who looks dignified and healthy despite high levels of sodium. We're talking salt and pepper dramatics here. Condiment-dispensing theater.

Born and largely reared in cowgirly Oklahoma (Montana makes a prettier surname, you've got to admit), Ruby (her birth name remains a secret) loved visiting her grandmother in Stillwater, who collected souvenir pitchers that she would eulogize for the grandchildren. "The pitchers all had stories," says Ruby. "I decided when I grew up, I wanted a house full of stories, too."

In 1974, having earned a music degree in classical French horn from the University of Michigan – "nobody offered me a scholarship to ride horses" – she moved to Seattle after drawing its name out of a hat. Presumably ten-gallon. She abandoned plans to study for a Ph.D. (Dr. Montana?) because Seattle was "too damn pretty," and took a job teaching school. By then she'd begun to collect tramp and folk art, some pieces of which became so valuable she felt obliged to sell them off. It wasn't long before she'd lassoed a house, painted it the tint of a stablegirl's first hickey, and was filling it with narratives of her own invention. "I'm in touch with everything in my house," she confides. "The furnishings are connected to my fantasy life and to my heart. They are my joy, my friends." And not just the nostalgic items. "We live in an age when most things feel like dental tools, although I do like modern objects if they have character."

She's also in touch with the sweet bird of youth. "Ceramics and cowgirl stuff are each a part of the child in me, and I'm interested in keeping that part alive. So many of the harsh realities of the adult world are unnecessary and absurd. People kill themselves because they're alienated from the child they really are."

Neither as flaky nor as flamboyant as you might suppose, Ruby comes across as the kindly enthusiastic schoolteacher she must have been. In pop culture, she searches for depth and meaning, not frivolity or escape. Her Pinto Pony is a gathering place for serious collectors and those attracted to the benevolently bizarre. Someday they may be able to ride the range with her as well. Ruby's professed ambition is to open a dude ranch. Complete with a personally decorated Roy Rogers suite – and a salt and pepper museum out back of the corral. Pink, no doubt. Like a twister of newborn mice, or a cowgirl's bubblegum cud.

House & Garden, 1991

Terence McKenna

From my downtown Seattle apartment, a number of provocative neon signs are visible, silently reciting themselves like lines from a hot, jerky poem. Above the entrance to the Champ Arcade, for example, there flashes the phrase LIVE GIRLS/ LIVE GIRLS/LIVE GIRLS, a sentiment that never fails to bring me joy, especially when I consider the alternative. Less jubilant, though more profound, is the sign in the dry cleaner's window. It signals simply, ALTERATIONS/ALTERATIONS/ ALTERATIONS, but it always reminds me of Terence McKenna – not merely because Terence McKenna is the leading authority on the experiential aspects of mind-*altering* plants, or because his lectures and workshops have *altered* my own thinking, but because Terence, perhaps more than anyone else in our culture, has the ability to let out the waist on the trousers of perception and raise the hemline of reality.

Scholar, theoretician, explorer, dreamer, pioneer, fanatic, and spellbinder, as well as ontological tailor, McKenna combines an erudite, if crackingly original, overview of history with a genuinely visionary approach to human destiny. The result is a cyclone of unorthodox ideas capable of lifting almost any brain out of its cognitive Kansas. When Hurricane Terence sets one's mind back down, however, one will find that it is on solid ground; for, far from Oz-built, the theories and speculations of

McKenna are rooted in a time-tested pragmatism thousands of years old. Many of his notions astonish us not because they are so new, but because they have been so long forgotten.

As the title of his collection *The Archaic Revival* implies, McKenna has found a key to the future in the dung heap of the past. (It is entirely appropriate to note that psychoactive mushrooms often sprout from cow pies.) During the European Renaissance, scientists, artists, and enlightened citizens turned back to a much older Greek civilization for the marble sparks with which to ignite their marvelous new bonfire. In more than one place in his collection of essays and conversations, McKenna is urging that we turn back – way, way back – to Paleolithic shamanism, to retrieve techniques that not only could ensure our survival, but could assist us in mounting a fresh golden age: in fact, *the* golden age, the one toward which the plot of all history has been building.

McKenna doesn't consider himself a shaman, although he has studied with shamans (and drunk their potent potions) in Asia and the Amazon. He says, however, that he is attempting to "explore reality with a shamanic spirit and by shamanic means." Indeed, the shaman's rattle buzzes hypnotically throughout his essays and lectures, although it is sometimes obscured by the whoosh of UFOs, for McKenna's imagination (and expertise) ranges from the jungle to hyperspace, and only a dolt would ever call him retro.

Here, let me squirt a few drops of Terence's essence into the punch bowl, so that we might sample the flavor and chart the ripples:

> My vision of the final human future is an effort to exteriorize the soul and interiorize the body, so that the exterior soul will exist as a superconducting lens of translinguistic matter generated out of the body of each of us at a critical juncture during our psychedelic bar mitzvah.

*

The problem with Christianity is it's the single most reactionary force in human history. I don't even know what is in second place, it's so far in front. And I believe that the destruction of paganism was probably the greatest disservice to the evolution of the human psyche that has ever been done. The repression of "witchcraft" is really the repression of botanical knowledge . . .

*

I don't believe that the world is made of quarks or electromagnetic waves, or stars, or planets, or any of these things. I believe the world is made of language.

*

If hallucinogens are operating as exopheromones, then the dynamic symbiotic relationship between primate and hallucinogenic plant is actually a transfer of information from one species to another.

*

Reality is a domain of codes, and that is why the UFO problem is like a grammatical problem – like a dangling participle in the fourth-dimensional language that makes reality. It eludes simple approaches because its nature is somehow embedded in the machinery of epistemic knowing itself.

*

I scoured India and could not convince myself that [its mysticism] wasn't a shell game of some sort or was any more real than the states manipulated by the various schools of New Age psychotherapy. But in the Amazon . . . you are conveyed into worlds that are appallingly different . . . [yet] more real than real.

These tiny sips from McKenna's gourd, served out of context and stripped of his usual droll garnishes, are nevertheless intoxicating and, to my mind, nourishing. In larger gulps, his brew may even heal the ulcers through which the modern world is bleeding.

Our problems today are more complex and more threatening than at any time in history. Sadly, we cannot even begin to solve those problems, because our reality orientations are lower than a snowman's blood pressure. We squint at existence through thick veils of personal and societal ignorance, overlaid with still more opaque sheets of disinformation, thoughtfully provided by the state, the church, and big business (often one and the same). The difference between us and Helen Keller is that she *knew* she was deaf and blind.

Radical problems call for radical solutions. Conventional politicians are too thickheaded to conceive of radical solutions and too fainthearted to implement them if they could, whereas political revolutionaries, no matter how well meaning, ultimately offer only bloodshed followed by another round of repression.

To truly alter conditions, we must alter ourselves – philosophically, psychologically, and perhaps biologically. The first step in those ALTERATIONS/ALTERATIONS/ALTERATIONS will consist mainly of cutting away the veils in order that we might see ourselves for that mysterious Other that we probably are and may always have been. Terence the Tailor has got the sharpest shears in town. And he's open Sundays and holidays. Once the veils are severed, we, each of us, can finally start to attend to our self-directed mutagenesis.

With his uniquely secular brand of eschatological euphoria, Terence McKenna is inviting us to a Doomsday we can live with. Be there or be squared.

Foreword to *The Archaic Revival*, HarperCollins, 1992

NOTE: When Terence McKenna was killed by a brain tumor in 2000 (a cruel irony considering the astonishing range and vibrancy of his cerebral equipment), his obituary in *The New York Times* reported that he had gone around predicting the "end of the world." This is patently false. What Terence talked about so convincingly and optimistically was a potential end of *history,* of our temporal paradigm – the end of a world system being a far different thing than the end of the world. It goes to show you that America's "newspaper of record" cannot always be trusted to get its facts straight, particularly when dealing with subjects that bloom outside the gray-walled garden of cultural orthodoxy.

Thomas Pynchon

Although I'm hypnotized by the colored lights he plays upon the dark waters of history – by the way he illuminates a shadowy ocean of conspiracies, atrocities, buffooneries, and arcana, causing it to sparkle in every direction – what I ultimately find thrilling and inspiring about Thomas Pynchon is an ostensibly far simpler thing. It's his choice of nouns.

His verbs, adverbs, and adjectives are engaging as well, but Pynchon is most impressive when he reaches into a vast bin of squirming language and somehow plucks out a noun that is fresh and unexpected, yet totally appropriate. For example, in *Mason & Dixon* he has the Reverend Cherrycoke (a splendid appellation!) wipe his bum with "a fistful of clover." A lesser writer might have settled for "grass" or "leaves" or "straw," none of which could have lit up the scene the way that *clover* does. It's small choices such as that one, choices to which, except subliminally, the general reader is oblivious, that tote the freight of genius.

Mark Twain opined that the difference between the perfect word and one that is merely adequate is the difference between lightning and a lightning bug. Well, move over, Zeus! Take to the storm cellar, ye firefly farmers! Thomas Pynchon has got both hands on the thunderbolt machine.

Bookforum, 2005

Debra Winger

She's walked a tightrope between fire and honey, between sulphur and roses, between sarcasm and succor, between monolith and disco ball, between hairshirt and hula skirt, between daunting daughter and doting mom, between the girl next door (gone a little bit wild) and international diva (with democratic sentiments). And now after marriage, maternity, and a relatively long hiatus from Hollywood, she's walking an unfamiliar line between fame and obscurity. She's walking down the creaky hallway of public memory.

Few who've ever heard it forget her voice – which sounds as if it's been strained through Bacall and Bogey's honeymoon sheets and then hosed down with plum brandy. Or her laugh – which sounds as if it's being squeezed out of a kangaroo bladder by a musical aborigine. Men remember her astride that mechanical bull in *Urban Cowboy* and fantasize about exchanging places with it. Women recall her salt-raw vulnerability in *Terms of Endearment* and issue wet sighs of identification.

Acquaintances and paparazzi, upon mention of her name, reminisce about her boyish Huck Finn swagger, her chain-saw intensity, her Algonquin-caliber wit. What the curious chroniclers of celebrityhood focus on, however, are the figure sixtynines she's allegedly skated on pond after pond of life's thin ice.

Starting at about sixteen, when she joined the Israeli army, then deserted to go on the bum in Paris, the Cleveland-born Valley girl sowed a fairly huge hopper of wild oats, it's true, though whether she was rowdier than her peers or just more imaginative is debatable; and though she isn't exactly sitting home these evenings knitting prayer shawls, it's been a long time since she's waltzed with the devil on a broken rail or rooted for jewels in the Andean snow. Nevertheless, it's hard to move out of one's pigeonhole, whether or not one ever signed a lease, and now as her film career resumes, the media's memories of her days as a saucy little troublemaker (don't those who insist on excellence always make trouble for those who're all too willing to settle for mediocrity?) obscure a more comprehensive picture of a woman whose complexities are as immense as her talents.

As for my personal recollections . . .

The first time I met Debra Winger, we spontaneously ducked out of a boring Tinseltown business meeting to take refuge in a dimly lit Santa Monica dive, where we caused the bartender to develop repetitive-motion disorder from the incessant refilling of our tequila glasses. Late in the day, as I recall, we borrowed a razor blade from the barkeep's kit, slit our thumbs, and exchanged blood by the light of the jukebox, bonding as siblings of a sort while we danced (illegally) to blues records and puffed Havana cigars. Memories are made of this.

Now, nine years later, and a mile or two southeast, we're sitting in a health hutch called I Love Juicy, sipping carrot froth and spinach squeezings like a couple of toothless old rabbits on a chlorophyll binge, and the only things bleeding are the beets in the blender.

While it's no secret that rehabilitation, recovery, and self-denial are the hallmarks of the American 90s, I'd like to believe that we've neither succumbed to trendy asceticism nor been born again as pea-pod puritans. I prefer to think we're cavorting with Bugs Bunny instead of José Cuervo because we're temporarily functioning somewhat below the summit of our physiological potential.

For more than six months, I've been blitzed by a mysterious virus that I took aboard on a pilgrimage to Timbuktu, while Winger is beset by environmental asthma she developed on a shoot in the dustlands of West Texas.

Thus afflicted, we hold celery stalks like pretend cigars while staring uneasily at the tape recorder that sits on the table next to our cabbage coolers. David Hirshey, brilliant editor and unwavering Winger fan (*he'll* never forget) has persuaded me to interview his dream girl for *Esquire,* to grill her about her recent return to the screen.

We're no more accustomed to relating in this formal way than we are to the lettucey libations of I Love Juicy, but we profess to be troupers, so, after much hesitation, I stub out my celery in an ashtray and switch on the machine.

"It's not fair," I begin. "How could a wise and loving God load up this vegetable juice with thousands of vitamins and not put a single one in tequila?"

Rising, as usual, to the occasion, Winger flashes me that ol' hellcat grin and says, "Oh, you can get nourishment from tequila, Tommy. But you have to eat the worm."

Esquire, 1993

STORIES, POEMS, & LYRICS

TRIPLETS

I went to Satan's house.
His mailbox was painted black.
A fleet of bonecrushers was parked in his driveway.
The thorns on his rosebushes were longer than shivs.
And sixty-six roosters scratched in his front yard, their
    spurs smoldering like cheap cigars.
I went to Satan's house.
It was supposed to be an Amway party.
I wanted one of those hard as hell steak knives.
The ones that can't tell the difference between mama's
    sponge cake and a chunk of rock cocaine.
I went to Satan's house.
I felt a little out of place.
But Satan's twin daughters soon put me at ease.
They tried on funny hats for me, showed me jewels,
    danced around my chair.
They read my fortune in a bowl of ashes, let me pet their
    Dobermans, and watch while they rinsed out their pink
    underthings.
I stopped by Satan's house,
I just happened to be in the neighborhood.
Satan came downstairs in a Raiders jacket.
His aura was like burnt rubber, but his grin could paint a
    sunrise on a coal shed wall.
"I see you've met Desire and Fulfillment," he said, pol-
    ishing his monocle with a blood-flecked rag.
"Regret is in the kitchen making coffee."

DREAM OF THE LANGUAGE WHEEL

Ancient elf bones
  stewing in the rain,
Angels the size of fruitflies
  circling a buddha turd,
Star maps drawn in lipstick
  on the mud walls of opium towns.

Images like those,
scenes such as these –

The red midgets of hell
  challenge Suzy's friends
  to a snowball fight
      Or
In the cave behind the waterfall
the ant king licks the clitoris
of the sleeping anthropologist. –

existing only on paper
are yet more important
than flags, bibles, gold,
guns and reputations.
    So
throw off your armor of acronyms,
your layers of numerical padding
    and
come bathe with me,
come slide beside me naked
into the world's steamy honeycomb
of words.

CATCH 28

The phantom arrived in a neon speedboat
ferrying a cargo
of coconuts and diamonds.

*

From the veranda of the malaria hotel
we saw it coming:
a kabuki magazine published by a hurricane.

*

Its clown-head prow sawed the surf in half
causing Crayola buddhas to run
over the hill with sacks of tadpoles on their backs.

*

A fat old tropical radio
interrupted the news to announce
that it was now king of the waterbugs.

*

Watching it turn wine into mink milk,
bedsheets into sandwiches of snow,
we imagined it must be a wind-up toy
designed by a mad scientist
to brighten the long frown of time.

*

But . . .
in the end
it was just my old mistress
and your new boss,
the moon.

THREE HAIKU

Brown spider dangling
from a single strand.
Up down, up down:
Zen yo-yo.

*

They've built their nests
in the chimneys of my heart,
those swallows that you lost.

*

Everywhere she walks,
that ghost is right behind her:
Ah, panty outline!

Moonlight Whoopee
Cushion Sonata

I

The witch-girl who lives by the bend in the river is said to keep a fart in a bottle.

It's a poisonous fart, green as cabbage, loud as a shotgun; and after moonset or before moonrise, her hut is illuminated by its pale mephitic glow. For a time, passersby thought she had television.

Of course, no antenna sprouts from her thatched roof, no satellite dish dwarfs her woodpile, and can you imagine the cable company stringing wires across the marsh and through the forest so that a witch-girl could watch the Occult Channel? Anyway, how would she pay for it? With the contents of her mushroom basket, the black candles she makes from hornet fat, her belladonna wine? With that cello she saws with a human bone?

It's conceivable that she could pay for it with her body: her body's been admired by many a fisherman who's chanced upon her wading the rapids in loonskin drawers. But no man's ever bought her body, and only one has had the courage to take it for free.

That fellow's gone away now. It's said he fled back to South

America and left her in the lurch. Oh, but she still has a hold on him, you can bet on that. Our witch-girl's got a definite hook in that fly-by-night romeo. She's woven his mustache hairs into a tiny noose. She's got his careless fart in a bottle by the stove.

II

Turn a mountain upside down, you have a woman. Turn a woman upside down, you have a valley. Turn a valley upside down, you get folk music.

In the old days, the men in our village played trombone. Some better than others, obviously, but most of the men could play. Only the males, sad to say. The women danced. It was the local custom. The practice has all but died out, though to this day, grizzled geezers are known to hide trombones under their beds at the nursing home. It's strictly forbidden, but late on summer nights, you can sometimes hear nostalgic if short-winded trombone riffs drifting out of the third-story windows, see silhouettes of old women on the second floor, dancing on swollen feet in fuzzy slippers or spinning in rhythmic circles in their wheelchairs.

As noted, however, our musical traditions have virtually vanished. Nowadays, people get their music from compact discs or FM radio. Who has time anymore to learn an instrument? Only the witch-girl by the bend in the river, sawing her cello with a human tibia, producing sounds like Stephen King's nervous system caught in a mousetrap.

When milk sours before it leaves the udder or grain starts to stink in the fields; when workers go out on strike at the sauerkraut factory, the missile base, or the new microchip plant down the road; when basements flood, lusty young wives get bedtime migraines, dogs wake up howling in the middle of the night, or the interference on TV is like a fight in

140

hot grease between corn flakes and a speedboat, people around here will say, "The witch-girl's playing her cello again."

Turn folk music upside down, you get mythology. Turn mythology upside down, you get history. Turn history upside down, you get religion, journalism, hysteria, and indecision.

III

The setting sun turned the river into a little red schoolhouse. Thus motivated, the frogs got to work conjugating their verbs. The witch-girl handled the arithmetic.

She divided a woodpecker by the square root of a telephone pole.

Multiplied the light in a fox's eyes by the number of umlauts on a Häagen-Dazs bar.

Added a kingfisher's nest to the Gross National Product.

Calculated the ratio of *duende* to pathos in the death song of a lamp-singed moth.

Subtracted a mallow from a marsh, an ant from an anthem, a buddha from a peach can shot full of holes.

IV

A white plastic bucket in a snowy field. A jackknife of geese scratching God's dark name in the sky. A wind that throbs but is silent. Candy wrappers silent against fence wire. Stags silent under their fright-wig menorahs. Bees silent in their science-fiction wax. A silent fiddle bow of blue smoke bobbing in the crooked chimney atop the witch-girl's shack.

It is on a cold, quiet Sunday afternoon past Christmas that the television crew arrives in our village. By suppertime, everybody but the hard cases at the nursing home knows it's in town. At the Chamber of Commerce breakfast Monday morning, hastily arranged to introduce the videopersons to the citizenry, the banquet room is overflowing. Understandably, we villagers assume the crew is here to film the new industries of which we are rightly proud. The director is diplomatic when he explains that missile bases and microchip plants are a dime a dozen.

"We are making a documentary on flatus," the director explains. The audience is spellbound.

"A normal human being expels flatus an average of fourteen times per day," he goes on to say. There is general muttering. Few would have thought the figure that high.

"We are speaking of all human beings, from babies in diapers to lawyers in three-piece suits. The mechanic billows the seat of his greasy coveralls, the glamorous movie actress poots through silk – and blames it on the maid or the Irish wolfhound. 'Naughty dog!'

"You people can do your math. That's eighty-four billion expulsions of flatus daily, worldwide, year after year. And that's just humans. Animals break wind, as well, so that wolfhound is *not* above suspicion. Anyway. We can explain reasonably well what flatus is: a gas composed primarily of hydrogen sulfide and varying amounts of methane. And whence it comes: generated in the alimentary canal by bacterial food waste, and vented through the anus. But where does it end up?"

Villagers look at one another, shake their heads.

"I won't trouble you today with environmental considerations, though I'm certain you can conceive of an upper atmospheric flatus layer, eating away at the ozone. This will be covered in our film. What I want to share with you is the difficulties we have encountered in trying to photograph the elusive trouser ghost, a genie as invisible as it is mischievous."

The director (a handsome man who wears a denim jacket and smokes a pipe) explains that attempts at spectrographic photography, while scientifically interesting, failed to produce an image with enough definition or optic impact to hold the attention of a lay viewer. And computer-generated animation seemed silly and fake. He goes on to explain how he and his staff fed a live model on popcorn, beer, and navy beans, then lowered her buttocks into a vat of syrup. Those of us who have just eaten pancakes for breakfast smile uneasily. "We got some marvelous bubbles," the director says, "but a gas bubble per se is not a fart."

"On Saturday, we heard from a reliable source that a resident of this community, or someone who lives nearby, has succeeded in actually netting a rectal comet and maintaining it intact. We were skeptical naturally, and on deadline, but also excited and a trifle desperate, so we impulsively dropped everything and traveled here at once. Now we are asking for your help. Does this person – and this preserved effluvium – exist? We were told only that the captor in question is some rich girl . . ."

"*Witch*-girl!" the audience cries out as one. Then, in gleeful unison – "Witch-girl" – they sing it out again.

* * * * * * * * * *

As for what happens next, the village is of two minds. The village, in fact, has split into a pair of warring camps. We have come to refer to the opposing factions as "Channel A" and "Channel B." Here are their respective versions.

CHANNEL A

A week passes. The television crew fails to return from the river. Suspecting foul play, the sheriff and his deputies tramp through the leafless forest and across the frozen bogs.

The witch-girl has disappeared. So have the director and his camerawoman. The audio technician is found sitting on a stump, a depraved glaze coating his eyes. When asked about the whereabouts of the others, the soundman mumbles, "The hole in the cheese." Over and over, "Hole in cheese. Hole in cheese." Until they take him away to a sanatorium. (Some joker at the feed store said they hoped it was a *Swiss* sanatorium.)

Eight months later, on Crooked Angle Island, a prospector stumbles across three skeletons, strangely intertwined. Inside the skull of each of them, rattling like a translucent jade acorn, is a perfectly crystallized fart.

CHANNEL B

The witch-girl is a big hit on PBS. Millions see her play the cello beside a bonfire, an owl perched on her shoulder. This has nothing to do with the subject of flatulence, but the director is obviously in her thrall.

She has a second fart-bottle on her nightstand now.

And throughout our township, television reception has significantly improved.

CODA

Perhaps it should be noted that sometime during this period, on an Argentine Independence Day, a notorious playboy fell to his death from one of the numerous gilded balconies of his Buenos Aires apartment. According to his mistress of the moment, he lost his balance while trying to capture with a gaucho hat a particularly volatile green spark that had escaped from a fireworks display in the plaza. *"Es mío!"* he cried as he went over the side. *It's mine.*

After Yesterday's Crash: The Avant-Pop Anthology, Penguin Books, 1995.

THE ORIGIN OF CIGARS

On the morning after the lunar eclipse,
she awoke with a funny feeling,
massaged her belly with hurricane drops,
rubbed barbecue sauce on her eyelids,
donned a necklace of alligator bones
and walked down to the Caribbee
where, asquat in a spice canoe,
she gave birth to a green banana.

"Not mine!" growled her husband,
pitching the new baby overboard
into the path of a barracuda,
who seized it like bait
just as lightning's alchemical zippo
ignited the infant's nib.

Transformed into a pufferfish,
the 'cuda was soon upstaging cookfires
as it puffed past the strand
in luxurious loopy-doops,
languid, masculine,
respiring like some kind of don
 – waiting for a cognac rain.

STICK INDIANS

You'll never really see them
and there's nothing left behind
to identify them in the labs
    of DNA.
And that footprint beneath your window
where in the night you saw the shadow
of a shadow of a shadow on the pane?
Just a heron with a gimpy leg
or some scarecrow run away
    to look for love.

When the owl suddenly freezes
on its perch atop the fir,
little ears cocked like nacho chips
    waiting for the cheese,
you yourself will listen hard
but only hear a scratching,
a clawing and a rasping
of the wind that wants to jimmy
    your locked door.

It's said they're a tribe of hermits
(whoever heard of such a thing?),
professors from the university
    of mud.
On paths of old mischief
they steal down from the hills,
bird nests for moccasins,
roadkill for their totem,
broken twigs like broken vowels
    spelling out their name.

While anthropology prays for day
to break and bring an end to nights
    it can't explain,
you have to ask "Where are they,
then, and are they any different
    from the rain?"
Well, they seem to have an interest
in all those things you do
when you suspect that no one
    is around.

And somehow you know they're out there
beyond the porch light's reach,
in the brambles,
in the hedge,
or out behind the woodpile
where they certainly appear
    to feel at home.
You imagine them raw and willowy,
you imagine them splintered and dry,
you imagine them witch brooms
    come to life.
But no matter how you picture them
or joke that they're your friends,
you can't begin to grasp the shtik
    of stick.

The Stick Indian casino
is in your skull
  – and you've already lost.

HOME MEDICINE

Last night
we attempted
a lint
transplant
but
her navel
rejected
it.

Clair de Lune

The old wolf trotted over the hill with a little pink heart in its teeth. A pattern appeared in the snow – a trail made by paws and tail and drops of candy-colored blood – and that pattern could be read as if it were a fairy tale, although the night was much too cold for fairies.

From behind a surf of clouds, the moon skitted into view like a boogie board. Cautiously, glancing left to right, the wolf set its treasure down on a fallen tree trunk, raised its muzzle toward the sky, and through dandelion parachutes of its own frozen breath, issued a long wail that sounded like the siren on a 6000-year-old ambulance.

Suddenly, the moon howled back.

For a long moment, the wolf held itself so still it might have been a cardboard cutout in a theater lobby (a sequel to *Dances with Wolves*, told from the animal's POV). The hairs of its mangy pelt were as erect as toy soldiers. Its eyes turned radioactive. Its breath was no longer visible. Its lame leg ached. Involuntarily, it pissed in the snow, affixing a new and perhaps not-so-happy ending to the fairy story previously written there. The old wolf waited.

As for the moon, it too was still, at rest on a cloudtop like some buttered skillet in which Vincent van Gogh was frying an egg.

Gradually, the lunar silence reassured the wolf, for while it, like its ancestors before it, had spent its life addressing each full moon without fail, it had never once, not even when a cub, expected or desired a reply. If there *was* a response, it resounded in the blood, in the spinal fluid, in the wolf juice, not the ears. Wolves did the vocalizing. Among beasts, as among men, the moon was understood to be mute.

But was it? Had the moon merely been biding its time all these years, patiently waiting for the right moment to make itself heard?

The wolf was straining so hard to learn what might have finally loosened the moon's tongue that it very nearly missed the small, squeaky voice that piped up only a few inches from its nose.

"Well," said the little heart, which had unobtrusively begun to beat again, puffing itself out like self-blowing bubblegum, "now that you've gotten the news, don't you think you ought to return me to the breast from which I was ripped?"

Although hungry and perplexed, and despite the fact that its conscience was as clean of guilt as a nun's bratwurst of mustard, the old wolf wearily complied, limping down the mountainside, squirming under the locked gate of the village, clambering atop a snowdrift, and stealing for the second time that night through a half-open nursery window.

And the next morning, my christening took place as scheduled.

ALOHA NUI

Drawn by the bloomy lights
of Honolulu,
the giant passenger moth
flies for a thousand miles,
through typhoon spray and volcano smoke,
sailors firing at it for sport,
barracuda snapping at its ass;
until, at last,
frazzled of antenna, salty of wing,
it wobbles into brief climactic orbit
around the 500-watt
coconut:
bachelor at a wedding
the bride never knew.

Are You Ready for the New Urban Fragrances?

(Headline in an Italian fashion magazine)

Yeah, I guess I'm ready, but listen:

Perfume is a disguise. Since the middle ages, we have worn masks of fruit and flower in order to conceal from ourselves the meaty essence of our humanity. We appreciate the sexual attractant of the rose, the ripeness of the orange, more than we honor our own ripe carnality.

Now, today, we want to perfume our cities, as well; to replace their stinging fumes of disturbed fossils' sleep with the scent of gardens and orchards. Yet, humans are not bees any more than they are blossoms. If we must pull an olfactory hood over our urban environment, let it be of a different nature.

I want to travel on a train that smells like snowflakes.

I want to sip in cafés that smell like comets.

I want to sleep in hotels that smell like the pheromones of sixteen-year-old girls.

Under the pressure of my step, I want the streets to emit the precise odor of a diamond necklace.

I want the newspapers I read to smell like the violins left in pawnshops by weeping hobos on Christmas Eve.

I want to carry luggage that reeks of the neurons in Einstein's brain.

I want a city's gases to smell like the golden belly hairs of the gods.

And when I gaze at a televised picture of the moon, I want to detect, from a distance of 239,000 miles, the aroma of fresh mozzarella.

HONKY-TONK ASTRONAUT
(Country song)

My wife up and left me a long time ago,
it's just as well that she's gone.
I've smoked out my windpipe with cheap cigarettes,
I can barely sing you this song.

But last night I saw more strange lights in the sky,
got so excited I thought I would die,
and it gave me the strength to go on.

I got a car with no brakes or transmission,
I usually travel by thumb.
Since I walked out on that job laying carpet
I've felt a bit like a bum.

But when I think of that great whirling saucer
and all the things it surely will offer,
my heart starts to beat like a drum.

Some people think I'm a leftover hippie,
    a loser, a drifter, or worse.
But I'm just a loner
    from Sedona, Arizona,
the center of the known universe.

I met a blonde in a bar up near Phoenix,
thought I'd found someone to love.
But when she laughed at me I climbed on a bridge,
hoping whiskey'd give me a shove –

– cause a cowboy with no job and no money

can't expect to convince any honey
that his friends rule the earth from above.

(SPOKEN)
The whole world's howling like a Tijuana dog,
everthing's a little bit insane.
Them spaceships had better hurry on down and get me,
before I drown in this hard-hearted rain.
But, hey, I just got the message
   that they're a-gonna,
they're a-gonna land right here
   in Sedona, Arizona,
And we can say adios to our pain.

Now some people think I'm a leftover hippie,
   a loser, a drifter, or worse.
But I'm just a loner
   from Sedona, Arizona,
The center of the known universe.

CREOLE DEBUTANTE

She went to the School of
                    Miss Crocodile,
learned to walk backwards,
skin a black cat with her teeth.
Soon, she could dance with
                    dead pirates,
cook perfect gumbo,
telephone the moon collect.
But it took 23 doctors to
                    fix her
after she kissed that Snake.

MASTER BO LING

Sinking his fingers
like rat fangs
into the round black cheese
(O moon that orbits Milwaukee!)
he heaves it onto
the path
the Tao
the waxy way
at whose end there awaits
amidst thunder
the ten buddhas.

R.S.V.P.

The invitation to
Tarzan's bar mitzvah,
written in nut juice
and wrapped in a leaf

Arrived in my mailbox
with an organic rustle,
smelling of chimp dung
but promising a feast

And evoking immediate
hot hoppy visions:
The hair of the cannibal
and the sweet of the beast

MY HEART IS NOT A POODLE
(Country song)

My love looks in the window and watches you sleep,
can't you hear it scratching at your door?
My love howls at the full moon down by the creek,
it ain't for sale in any store.

My love is a wild thing and it can't be trained
to do tricks to entertain your group
so put away that leash and that hoop:
my heart is not a poodle.

My love is wild, hog wild,
it ain't for a sissy or a child,
it's the hot stuff, not the mild,
don't treat it like a poodle.

You can housebreak your puppy, you can housebreak your
   cat
you can even housebreak some bunny rabbits.
You can teach some old boys to wipe their boots on a mat,
but love holds on to its bad habits.

Passion hides in the shadows where it's damp and it's dark
to sneak out and bite you on the leg.
No, it won't sit up and beg:
My heart is not a poodle.

My love is wild, hog wild,
it ain't for a sissy or a child,
it's sweet but it's also vile,
don't mistake it for no poodle.

Real love likes to run free like a fox or a cur,
it ain't looking for no master,
so don't be tying no fancy ribbons 'round its neck
or it's gonna run all the faster.
I like the way you look, baby, I love how you smell
I long to be your very own,
but don't toss me no old bone;
my heart is not a poodle.

My love is wild, hog wild,
it ain't for a sissy or a child,
it's the hot stuff, not the mild,
don't treat it like a poodle.

(SPOKEN)
It ain't nobody's lapdog.
Won't wear no rhinestone collar.
Don't even think about calling it "Fifi."

WEST TO SATORI

The meditation mat
is the yogi's horse:
Git along little yoga,
gotta reach
El Snuffing Out Candle
afore sundown
        own
          own
            own
              own.

WILD CARD

Between the ace and the trey
between the raise and the fold
between the hat and the wand
down and dirty in Vegas
or up a magician's silky sleeve,
the red deuce bides its time.

Born under the sign of Gemini
on Groundhog Day in Baden Baden,
bipolar double agent
too wild for just one world:
two hearts beating
   in one pale breast,
diamonds the color of rubies dangling
   from the Devil's lobes,
Euclidean tomatoes,
jigsaw pasties,
Rasputin and his clone
in velvet suits
   scheming to topple a royal house,
Saint Valentine's testicles swaying
imperceptibly to the fickle rhythms
   of chance:
the sagacious player understands
that these are no mere figures of speech.

If some night a pair
   of bloodshot eyes
stare unblinking into yours,
remember:
no hand is a winning hand

'til you dare to lay it down,
and He who made the red deuce
   wild
knows both your secret names.

OPEN WIDE

Jacking the molar free
of its purchase in the bark-blackened gums,
the mission dentist made to toss it
into a pail of slops –
but the shaman seized it,
licked it lovingly clean of his own blood,
used a baby monkey to buff it,
built a wooden cage for it
and set it next to the dream pole
in the center of the village.

At sunrise the next morning
the tooth commenced to sing
in a sweet little Gloria Estefan voice,
awakening the missionary
who, chronically dazed by everything around him
for a hundred miles,
turned to the first page in his stiff hymnal
and tried to join in.

TWO FOR MY YOUNG SON

I

If Frankenstein grows tomatoes
And Dracula farms beans,
If the Wolfman plants the croutons
That Kong puts on his greens,
If the Creature From the Black Lagoon
Loves carrots, peas, and hash,
If Godzilla peels the potatoes
Used in the Monster Mash,
If Vego the Giant Cauliflower
Eats people like a fiend,
Then what is keeping you, my son,
From licking your plate clean?

II

The Abominable Snowman
Lives far from any city
Up in the Himalayas
Where snow falls like confetti.
Men climb far to look for him
Their ropes coiled like spaghetti
But though they've looked for years and years
They haven't found him, yeti.

The Towers of St. Ignatz
A script treatment for a feature film

Freddie Manhattan is a rock star of moderate magnitude – he has an asteroid talent but a supernova ego. He has just been informed by his manager that he'll be cutting his new album in N.Y. right after the Christmas holidays (late autumn lies like a frosty leaf upon America). Freddie's in a snit. N.Y. January is colder than penguin toejam. Okay, okay, L.A., then. No! Freddie wants the Caribbean. Elton John records in the Caribbean, Sting records in the Caribbean, the Caribbean is good enough for Mick Jagger, it ought to be good enough for Freddie Manhattan. Exasperated, the manager says he'll see what he can do.

In Minneapolis, meanwhile, Howard, a high-school history teacher, is visiting a former colleague, one Newton Beck. A biology teacher, Newton, thirty-one, got one of his students pregnant. Even though he married the girl, he was fired. Young Mrs. Beck gave birth to twin sons, now about six months old. The twins are fraternal (non-identical) and Newton is explaining to Howard the ways in which they differ, one from the other. Heidi Beck seems uninterested in the Beck twins, her husband, or his guest. She is dancing alone to a Freddie Manhattan album.

Freddie, back in N.Y., is watching the weather on TV. "It's already fuckin' snowing in Minneapolis," he observes sourly.

As dawn breaks the next day, the twins begin to fret. Newton gets up and heats their formula. It's still early when they are fed so he slides back in bed with his teenaged bride and instigates some industrial strength foreplay. Heidi claims she's too sleepy. Newton rolls over and peeks through the blinds. A light snow, the first of the season, has fallen during the night. "At least I'll have something new to do at work today," he says.

Newton now works as a guide at the Twin Cities Museum of Natural History. On a day like today, as a part of the Wonders of the Universe tour, he will collect fresh snowflakes and project them upon a screen to demonstrate both the intricate beauty of crystal structure and the infinite variety of nature: "Of all the trillions upon trillions of snowflakes that have fallen upon the earth, no two have ever been alike."

Freddie's manager is on the phone to the Caribbean recording studio, arguing about rental time. "Freddie can't pay what Elton pays. He doesn't move as much product as Elton moves. Only don't tell him that."

Just before the final guided tour of the day, Newton calls Heidi. She complains that the twins are not taking their nap. "How can they sleep with that music up so loud?" he asks, referring to the blare of one of Freddie Manhattan's recent CDs. Once more, he collects and projects some snowflakes. "Of all the trillions and trillions . . ." The visitors laugh. They think it's a joke. It takes Newton a while to really focus on the fact that two of the projected snowflakes are absolutely identical! He almost faints from astonishment.

Newton's life is dramatically transformed. He quickly becomes obsessed with the implications of the identical flakes (which he managed to photograph just as they began to melt). While Heidi practices on her guitar, Newton studies the flake pictures, examines thousands of new flakes, meditates on the meaning of it all – does this mean that certain previously inviolable laws of nature are now in question, or is it simply an amazing coincidence without planetary or cosmic significance? – and broods because neither the scientific community nor the public is as excited about it as he is. Minneapolis TV stations give him a few minutes of exposure, but interest quickly fades, and serious scientists treat the photos as if they're some kind of hoax.

Due to his obsession, Newton's in trouble at work. And in more trouble than usual at home. Heidi now thinks he's crazy as well as old. Then, a telegram arrives from the editor-publisher at the *Weekly World Enquirer,* offering to pay $300 for exclusive rights to the flake pix. Heidi says ask for $500. Howard (the history teacher) advises against it altogether. Newton decides to hand carry the picture to *W.W.E.* offices in Miami, so that he might convince the editor to publish a lengthy article. Sleazy publicity is better than no publicity at all. He dumps baby clothes out of Heidi's guitar case, throws in a change of underwear and the pictures. He buys a bus ticket to Miami.

On the island of St. Ignatz, Freddie is cutting his album. At about four a.m., there's a break at the studio and Freddie walks outside in the moonlight to have a smoke. Two wild-looking Rastaesque black men come out of the jungle, subdue him, and carry him off.

Early the next morning, Freighter and his common-law wife, Cookie, are awakened by a terrible racket. Freighter is a middle-aged white American, a burly, bald giant with sailor tattoos and a red beard. Cookie is a cute, young black woman. Bleary-eyed, Freighter stumbles out of his picturesque shack to see what the hell is going on. Across the clearing, at the equally quaint shack of Zumba, Zumba's wife, Leroyette, and his brother, Brutha (the location is far back in the hills and nobody else lives within five or six miles), Freddie has been chained to a post in the dirt yard. He has been given a cheap, tinny electric guitar (wired to a car battery), and ordered to perform.

Freddie is bitching and moaning, not so much at the command performance, as at the quality of the guitar. Freighter stares dumbfounded at the scene. Zumba wears a fiercely triumphant grin.

Each of the two shacks has an unusually tall, makeshift, eccentric antenna attached to it. The antennae appear to have been built in stages, out of whatever material (mostly junk) that happened to be available at the time of each addition. These twin towers are maybe forty feet high and rather bizarre. Cookie looks from Freighter to the towers to Freddie and back to Freighter again. She is apprehensive about something.

Arriving at the *Weekly World Enquirer* office in Miami, Newton catches the publishing tycoon who had wired him, Desmond Hinkley Jr., on his way out the door. Hinkley Jr. (he insists on the Jr. – if you call him Mr. Hinkley, he corrects you: "Mr. Hinkley *Junior*") has received a tip that something has happened to Freddie Manhattan down on St. Ignatz Island, and he's on his way there in hopes of a scoop. Newton refuses to hand over the snowflake pictures without an interview. Hinkley Jr., in a rush, offers to hear him out aboard his Lear jet, so Newton tags along to the Caribbean.

High above the ground, Freighter is adding to the height of his antenna tower. He keeps glancing down at Zumba, but Zumba is ignoring him. Zumba stands with his arms smugly folded, enjoying Freddie's forced concert. Freighter yells down to Cookie to turn up the music on his shortwave, but it's already at full volume and it can't compete with Freddie's live performance. Freighter fumes and Cookie looks worried.

In his hotel room, Hinkley Jr. is on the phone dictating his scoop on the Freddie Manhattan kidnapping. He instructs his subordinates that once they've broken the story, they are to announce that Hinkley Jr. is personally organizing and leading a rescue mission. He'll leave at first light. Meanwhile, that snowflake freak, Newton Beck, is keeping a watch on the recording studio and will alert the paper immediately should a ransom demand be made.

At the secret clearing, Cookie's fears have materialized. During the night, Freighter has gone off in the dune buggy. Now he squeals up in front of the shack – and discharges his prize: Newton. His triumph quickly turns into humiliation when Newton backs up his insistence that he's not a rock star by opening his guitar case.

"It's snow," Newton says. "You know what snow is?" At first, they believe he's talking about cocaine and start to rough him up. When it's demonstrated that he possesses neither an instrument nor drugs, but merely some boring photographs, Zumba and Brutha have a great, long laugh at Freighter's expense. Freighter stalks away to sulk, and Newton tells the story to the rest of them, including Freddie. (It's here that we learn the details of Newton's affair with Heidi.) Cookie is the most attentive. Her eyes light up when she hears about the twins. After the rest of them have wandered off, she stays.

Cookie tells Newton about the obsessive competition between Freighter and Zumba. It is mostly manifest in the radio towers: every time Zumba makes an addition, Freighter adds to his tower (originally, they were trying to see who could get the best reception of Miami rock stations but they have moved well beyond function into pure form). Recently, Leroyette has become pregnant, so Freighter, competitively, is trying desperately to impregnate Cookie.

Well and good, but all that interests Newton is solving the mystery of the identical snowflakes, and here he is chained to a post in the isolated interior of a backward island, helpless to act upon his breathtaking discovery. Even were he free in the civilized world, however, he would be at a loss to solve the mystery, since science preferred to ignore his discovery, to deny its implications. Cookie listens attentively. Then, as she gets up to go inside (where Freighter is wailing for her), she says, softly, "I knows somebody who might can hep you."

Late that night, Cookie slips out and unchains Newton. By moonlight, she leads him into the jungle. After a long trek, they look down upon a shack by a waterfall. " 'Fore you go down there you be doin' something for me, Mr. Twinmaker." Newton resists, telling her that he knows nothing about making twins, that it was an accident of nature. Cookie seduces him anyway, and there follows a brief but energetic act of coitus beneath a mango tree.

Afterwards, she takes him to the shack, where their knock is answered by a woman wearing heavy beads, gobs of bright red lipstick, and smoking a big cigar. A black rooster is cradled in her arms. She is stroking it.

Cookie leaves Newton with her mother. Mama Lo's shack is dominated by an ornate shrine, in the center of which are lurid pictures of Jesus and Mary. Mama Lo makes Newton puff her cigar. He gets dizzy. With a short cord, Mama Lo ties the rooster to Newton's ankle. When he looks up, the pictures of Jesus and Mary are gone and the photo of the identical snowflakes has been pinned up in their place. Once again, Mama Lo passes him the stogy.

Meanwhile, Desmond Hinkley Jr. and his ragtag search party of tourists, rock musicians, and local black policemen have rousted the inhabitants of a mountain village, and, holding aloft Freddie Manhattan albums, are unsuccessfully questioning them. The villagers are sullen. Not a peep. Lionel, the cop who is acting as Hinkley Jr.'s chief aide, announces that clearly it must be Zumba who is responsible for the abduction. According to Lionel, this folk hero, Zumba, and his brother reside – he points to a map – deep in the valley between the twin volcanoes. [NOTE: the island of Montserrat, site of George Martin's recording studio, is, indeed, dominated by twin volcanoes.] It is only about fifteen miles from the village. "We'll be there in no time," Hinkley Jr. encourages his men. But when they return to their two vehicles, they find the tires have been slashed. They'll have to hike.

"What I want to know," Newton confides to Mama Lo, "is whether the snowflake phenomenon is a signal that the Earth is about to enter a new phase of evolutionary development, one in which many traditional scientific truisms will become obsolete, or have we simply been wrong all along in our rigid assumptions regarding the structure of reality." Mama instructs him to shut up and enjoy the cigar. A faint blue glow has begun to emanate from the shrine.

At the clearing, Freighter discovers that Cookie has freed Newton. "What do it matter?" Cookie asks. "He couldn't play no music no how." "Zumba has a worthless brother," Freighter says. "I don't have no worthless brother. He was gonna be my worthless brother." "Well," says Cookie, "he not you brother." She turns from him, smiles to herself, and places her hands over her womb. "And he not so worthless."

Freddie, meanwhile, pleads, whines, and threatens. Until Zumba swings a machete a few inches from his nose. Then he sings and plays. Zumba grins contentedly. Brutha joins in on the bongos. This routine is repeated throughout the day.

Hinkley Jr.'s rescue party sweats and pants up the steep jungle road. A bit of bravado has drained from its leader.

The strange blue light has completely enveloped Mama Lo's shack. Newton writhes on a straw mat on the floor. His eyes are closed. He groans, he writhes.

Several feet of snow blankets Minneapolis. As a Freddie Manhattan album plays on the stereo, a melancholy Heidi stares out the window. In the distance, a small figure hops across the snowy suburban landscape. As it nears, we see the figure is Newton. He is bound with rope, as if to a mast, to a giant chicken leg. No chicken, just the leg. The leg hops through the snow, toward the house. In their crib, the twins begin to cry. Heidi picks them up, wraps them well, and carries them outside. As they stand in the snow, the chicken leg hops around them. Newton blows kisses at the three of them. The twins goo and smile. Heidi mouths halfhearted kisses at Newton. Then, the chicken leg carries him off into the distance. He disappears beyond the pale horizon.

At kiosks all over America, the *Weekly World Enquirer* reveals the news of Freddie's abduction. Network TV picks it up. The word "terrorists" is used. Dan Rather, a bit bemused, announces that tabloid publisher Desmond Hinkley Jr. is leading a rescue party in the St. Ignatz interior.

Indeed he is. But not without difficulty. Hinkley Jr. and Lionel, dirty, hot, and tired, look at one another. They agree they must be lost.

Things are quiet at the clearing. Freddie plucks gently at the silly guitar, Brutha beats the bongos ever so softly. Zumba is speaking philosophically. White men, black men seem like twins, he says. Fraternal twins. They look alike, in some ways, but there are many differences. Like the biblical twins, Jacob and Esau, they are separated by inequalities, destined to live apart.

While Zumba speaks, Freighter drives up in the dune buggy. He has been to the recording studio and stolen Freddie's personal guitar. "My ax!" exclaims Freddie. He hurls the cheap guitar to the ground and embraces his beloved instrument. Zumba ignores all this. He continues his monologue. The twin souls of black and white, rich and poor, socialist and capitalist, can never be joined, Zumba says. He pauses. "Except, maybe, by music."

Mama Lo is singing to Newton. All the while, she is swinging before his glazed eyes a corkscrew on the end of a string. Back and forth, pendulum-like. Newton's gaze moves along the spiral of the corkscrew, following it down, down, down . . .

With Newton still bound to it, the giant chicken leg hops up the slope of the first volcano. It hops over the edge and down into the crater. Inside the volcano, the music is very loud. Upon a ledge, the Goddess is standing. She is resplendent, beautiful, both funky and ethereal. In her hands are a pair of dice. The Goddess shakes the dice and throws them. The dice are normal size when they leave her hand, but when they hit the volcano floor, they are huge. One large die lands at the foot of the chicken leg. Newton looks down upon it, sees it is a 2. The second die rolls to a stop beside it. This one is a 3.

As Newton stares, the two spots on the first die are replaced with the faces of his twin boys. He turns to the second die, whose three spots are just changing into the faces of three racially mixed baby girls. Each has a different-colored ribbon in her hair. The three primary colors.

Suddenly, the chicken leg hops into an underground passage. As it moves along the lava corridor (the primordial soup is bubbling, spattering Newton; it is red and looks suspiciously like barbecue sauce), we cut to an aerial view of the twin volcanoes. There is a roar, and a puff of smoke and steam erupts from the second volcano. Out of it pops Newton aboard the chicken leg, only now it is a cooked drumstick, dripping barbecue sauce. Newton gets a spectacular view of the island and its twin volcanic peaks.

In front of the shrine, Newton's head snaps. He "comes to." With a bewildered expression, he looks at Mama Lo. His attention is directed to the shrine. Where the snowflake picture was is now the face of the Goddess. The Goddess smiles and speaks, directly to Newton. "The dice are always rolling," is what she says.

As Newton turns to Mama Lo, as if to speak, the shack door is smashed, and in bursts Hinkley Jr. and his posse. "You're saved!" Hinkley Jr. yells to Newton. To Mama Lo he shouts, "No false moves! In the name of the *Weekly World Enquirer* and free men everywhere, you're under arrest!"

A violent tropical thunderstorm has moved in over the clearing. Taking refuge from the downpour, Zumba, Brutha, Leroyette, and Freddie (unchained) are under Zumba's shack, relaxing and smoking spliffs. Freighter, however, has climbed to the top of his antenna tower, where he is wiring Freddie's expensive and adored guitar to the tip. When Freddie sees this, he runs out into the storm, jumping up and down and screaming. A distraught Cookie stands in the rain, yelling at Freighter to come down. "I got to beat him," growls Freighter. "Honey, we *is* going to beat him," says Cookie, rubbing her belly.

A bolt of lightning strikes Zumba's tower. It sparks across the clearing, joining, momentarily, the twin towers with an electric arc. Freighter receives a jolt that knocks him off of his lofty perch.

In Minneapolis, Heidi is watching TV. The newscaster says that Freddie fans are gathering in Miami, keeping a vigil. Heidi says to the twins, "I wish we'd gone to Miami with your weird old daddy."

When Hinkley Jr.'s party, including Newton, arrives at the clearing, the rain has just stopped. Unconscious, Freighter lies on the wet ground. Zumba and Freddie are working over him. Newton offers to drive to the civilized part of the island and fetch a doctor. He speeds away in the dune buggy. At one point, he can make out in the distance the waterfall and Mama Lo's shack. He slows down and almost stops, but drives on.

A few days later, a Lear jet lands in Miami and Freddie Manhattan deplanes. The media is there in full force, as well as several hundred cheering fans. Some fans are carrying a huge banner, reading: WELCOME HOME FREDDIE! Among the fans is Heidi. She lays the twins on a baggage cart and moves in to touch Freddie. There is instantly something between them. Freddie looks her over and we can virtually hear the chemical crackle.

Newton, who has deplaned after Freddie (and after Hinkley Jr., now monopolizing the media), picks up the twins and walks slowly away with them. Heidi glances over, sees this, hesitates, then moves back into Freddie's arms.

Nearly a year passes. It is early winter in Minneapolis. Newton drives through the snow to a day care center, where he deposits the twins. He then drives on to work. At the museum, a letter awaits him. It bears a St. Ignatz postmark. On the way to his station, he tears it open. He removes two photos. Walking, he looks at the first. It's a picture of Zumba and Leroyette. They have a baby boy.

As Newton lectures, we see the second photo, which he has just taped to his projector. Cookie and Freighter (Freighter has a wooden leg now, and is making a "V" for Victory sign) are holding triplets: three little racially mixed girls, each with a different colored bow in her hair.

"Of all the trillions and trillions of snowflakes that have fallen upon the Earth, scientists *claim* no two . . ."

Newton breaks off. He stares at the photo of his triplets. As he projects fresh snowflakes onto a screen, he takes up again. ". . . scientists *claim* no two have ever been alike. However, folks, as we know, the dice are always rolling." Expectantly, he turns to examine the screen.

Ergo! magazine, 1990

MUSINGS & CRITIQUES

In Defiance of Gravity
Writing, Wisdom, &
The Fabulous Club Gemini

I

It had been a long time since I'd contemplated suicide. In fact, I don't believe I'd ever before considered the corporal delete key an option. Yet there I was, teetering on a bridge high above some oyster-lit backwater from Puget Sound, thinking about closing my earthly accounts with a leap and a splash.

Why? My romantic life couldn't have been sweeter, my health was close to rosy, the writing was going well, finances were adequate, and while the horror show that that cupidinous cult of corporate vampires was making of our federal government might be enough to drive me to drink (a trip I'm seldom reluctant to take), the political knavery does not exist that could drive me *into* the drink. No, the truth is, I was being prodded to execute a Kevorkian header into the Stygian slough by a short story I'd just read in a back issue of *The New Yorker*.

Entitled (ironically enough) *Fun With Problems,* the piece was composed by Robert Stone, and you can bet it wasn't Stone's prose style that had weakened my will to live: the man's a crack technician whose choices of verb and adjective can sometimes floor me with admiration. He's a smithery of a storyteller who's hammered out a stalwart oeuvre – but holy Chernobyl, is he bleak! Stone apparently believes the human condition one pathetically unstable, appallingly corrupt piece of business, and, frankly, at this stage of our evolutionary development there's a shortage of evidence to contradict him. Nevertheless, I'd always counted myself among those free spirits who refuse to allow mankind's ignoble deportment and dumb-cluck diatheses to cloud their grand perspective or sleet on their parade. On that day, however, Stone's narrative prowess had been such as to infect me (unconscionably, I now contend) with his Weltschmerz.

In fairness, Stone alone was not to blame. For too many years my edacious reading habits had been leading me into one unappealing corner after another, dank cul-de-sacs littered with tear-stained diaries, empty pill bottles, bulging briefcases, broken vows, humdrum phrases, sociological swab samples, and the (lovely?) bones of dismembered children: the detritus of a literary scene that, with several notable exceptions, has been about as entertaining as a Taliban theme park and as elevating as the prayer breakfast at the Bates Motel. *Fun With Problems* was simply the final straw, the charred cherry atop a mad-cow sundae.

So, who knows how things might have turned out that glum afternoon had not I suddenly heard, as I flirted with extinction, a particular sound in my mind's ear; the sound, believe it or not, of a distant kitty cat; a sound that instantly transported me away from the lure of fatal waters, away from the toxic contagions of sordid fiction, and into a place – a real place, though I've only visited it in my imagination – a place called the Fabulous Club Gemini.

II

The Fabulous Club Gemini. Where is it, anyhow? Memphis, probably. Or Houston. No, actually I think it might be one of the ideologically unencumbered features of Washington, D.C. In any case, some years back, a music writer for the *Village Voice* made a pilgrimage to the smoke-polluted, windowless, cinderblock venue, wherever its exact location, and while being introduced to some of the ancient musicians who'd been playing the Fabulous Club Gemini practically since the vagitus of time, the pilgrim became so excited he momentarily lost his downtown cool.

"I can't believe," he quoted himself as having gushed, "that I'm talking to the man who barked on Big Mama Thornton's recording of 'Hound Dog'!"

"Yeah," the grizzled sideman drawled. "I was gonna *meow* – but it was too hip for 'em."

Okay, perhaps I'm overly fanciful, but I have reason to suspect it might have been precisely an echo from that crusty confession that, as incongruous as it may seem, enticed me down from the kamikaze viaduct. I do know that I'm often reminded of it when I glance at the annual lists of Pulitzers, Booker Prizes, or National Book Awards; when an interviewer's question forces me to re-examine my personal literary aesthetic; or when speaking with eager students in those university creative writing programs where prescribed, if rarified, barking is actively promoted and any feline departure summarily euthanized.

There's some validity, I suppose, in the academic approach, for as Big Mama's accompanist would attest, our culture simply has a far greater demand for the predictable bow-wow than for the unexpected caterwaul: orthodox woofing pays the rent. In a dogma-eat-dogma world, a few teachers, editors, and critics may be hip enough to tolerate a subversive mew, a quirky purr now and again, but they're well aware of the fate that awaits those who produce – or sanction – mysterious off-the-wall meowing when familiar yaps and snarls are clearly called for.

Let me explain that when I refer to "meowing" here, what I'm really talking about is the human impulse to be playful; an impulse all too frequently demeaned and suppressed in the adult population, especially when it manifests itself in an unconventional manner or inappropriate context. To bark at the end of a song entitled "Hound Dog" is just playful enough to elicit a soupçon of mainstream amusement, but Fred (I believe that was the sessionman's name), in wanting instead to meow, was pushing the envelope and raising the stakes, raising them to a "hipper" level perhaps, a more irreverent level undoubtedly. There's a sense in which ol' Fred was showing a tiny spark of what the Tibetans call "crazy wisdom," a sense in which he was assuming for a bare instant the archetypal role of the holy fool.

Now, the fact that Fred would have denied any such arcane ambition, the fact that he may only have been stoned out of his gourd at the time, all that is irrelevant.

It's also unimportant that Fred's recording studio tom-foolery lacked real profundity, that while it may have been eccentrically playful it was not very *seriously* playful. What does matter is that we come to recognize that playfulness, as a philosophical stance, can be very serious, indeed; and, more-over, that it possesses an unfailing capacity to arouse ridicule and hostility in those among us who crave certainty, reverence, and restraint.

The fact that playfulness – a kind of *divine* playfulness intended to lighten man's existential burden and promote what Joseph Campbell called "the rapture of being alive" – lies near the core of Zen, Taoist, Sufi, and Tantric teachings is lost on most westerners: working stiffs and intellectuals alike. Even scholars who acknowledge the playful undertone in those disciplines treat it with condescension and disrespect, never mind that it's a worldview arrived at after millennia of exhaustive study, deep meditation, unflinching observation, and intense debate.

Tell an editor at *The New York Review of Books* that Abbott Chögyam Trungpa would squirt his disciples with water pistols when they became overly earnest in their meditative practice, or that the house of Japan's most venerated ninja is filled with Mickey Mouse memorabilia, and you'll witness an eye-roll of silent-movie proportions. Like that fusty old patriarch in the Bible, when they become a man (or woman), they "put away childish things," which is to say they seal off with the hard gray wax of fear and pomposity that aspect of their being that once was attuned to wonder.

As a result of their having abandoned that part of human nature that is potentially most transcendent, it's no surprise that modern intellectuals dismiss playfulness – especially when it dares to present itself in literature, philosophy, or art – as frivolous or whimsical. Men who wear bow ties to work every day (let's make an exception for waiters and Pee-wee Herman), men whose dreams have been usurped either by the shallow aspirations of the marketplace or the drab clichés of Marxist realpolitik, such men are not adroit at distinguishing that which is lighthearted from that which is merely lightweight. God knows what confused thunders might rumble in their sinuses were they to encounter a concept such as "crazy wisdom."

Crazy wisdom is, of course, the opposite of conventional wisdom. It is wisdom that deliberately swims against the current in order to avoid being swept along in the numbing wake of bourgeois compromise, wisdom that flouts taboos in order to undermine their power; wisdom that evolves when one, while refusing to avert one's gaze from the sorrows and injustices of the world, insists on joy in spite of everything; wisdom that embraces risk and eschews security, wisdom that turns the tables on neurosis by lampooning it, the wisdom of those who neither seek authority nor willingly submit to it.

Oddly enough, one of the most striking illustrations of crazy wisdom in all of western literature occurs in a pedestrian piece of police pulp by Joseph Wambaugh. *The Black Marble* is so stylistically lifeless it could have been printed in embalming fluid, but the rigor mortis of its prose is temporarily enlivened by a scattering of scenes that I shall attempt to summarize (although it's been decades since I read the book).

As I remember it, a relatively inexperienced member of the Los Angeles Police Department is transferred to the vice squad. No sooner does the new cop report for duty than he's introduced to a strange lottery. There is, it seems, an undesirable beat, a section of the city that no vice cop ever wants to patrol. It's a sleazy, filthy, volatile, extremely dangerous area, full of shooting galleries and dark alleys and not a donut shop in sight. So great has been the objection to being assigned to that sinister beat that the precinct captain has devised a raffle to cope with it. At the beginning of each night shift, he produces a bag of marbles, every marble white save one. One by one, the cops reach in the bag and pull out their fate. The unfortunate who draws the single black marble must screw up his spine and descend that evening into the urban hell.

Around the drawing of the marbles there's a considerable amount of tension, and the new man quickly succumbs to it. Just showing up for work is twice as stressful as it ought to be. In the station house, negativity is prevalent, jovial camaraderie rare.

The new cop draws the black marble a couple of times and finds the dreaded zone to be as violent and unsavory as advertised. However, he not only survives there, he learns he can tolerate the beat reasonably well by changing his attitude toward it, by regarding it less as a tribulation than as some special opportunity to escape routine and regularity, by appreciating it as an unusual experience available to very few people on the planet. Slowly, his anxiety begins to evaporate.

One night he shocks his comrades by emptying the bag and *deliberately* selecting the black marble. The next night, he does it again. From then on, he simply strolls into the station and nonchalantly requests the black marble. He no longer has to fret over the possibility of losing the draw. For better or worse, he controls his destiny.

Ordeal now has been transformed into adventure, stress into excitement. The transformer is himself transformed, his uptightness replaced first by a kind of giddy rush, then by a buddhistic calm. Moreover, his daring, his abandon, his serenity, is contagious. Vice squad headquarters gradually relaxes. Liberated, the whole damn place opens up to life.

And that, brothers and sisters, though Wambaugh probably didn't intend it, is crazy wisdom in action.

Admittedly, when the cop made the short straw his own, when he seized the nasty end of the stick and rode it to transcendence, he put himself in extra peril. That's par for the course. Only an airhead would mistake the left-handed path for a safe path.

While serious playfulness may be an effective means of domesticating fear and pain, it's not about meowing past the graveyard. No, the seriously playful individual meows right through the graveyard gate, meows into his or her very grave. When Oscar Wilde allegedly gestured at the garish wallpaper in his cheap Parisian hotel room and announced with his dying breath, "Either it goes or I go," he was exhibiting something beyond an irrepressibly brilliant wit. Freud, you see, wasn't whistling "Edelweiss" when he wrote that gallows humor is indicative of "a greatness of soul."

The quips of the condemned prisoner or dying patient tower dramatically above, say, sallies on TV sitcoms by reason of their gloriously inappropriate refusal, even at life's most acute moment, to surrender to despair. The man who jokes in the executioner's face can be destroyed but never defeated.

When a venerable Zen master, upon hearing a sudden burst of squirrel chatter outside his window, sat up in his deathbed and proclaimed, *"That's* what it was all about!", his last words surpassed Wilde's in playful significance, constituting as they did a koan of sorts, an enigmatic invitation to rethink the meaning of existence. Anecdotes such as this one remind the nimble-minded that there's often a thin line between the comic and the cosmic, and that on that frontier can be found the doorway to psychic rebirth.

Ancient Egyptians believed that when a person died, the gods immediately placed his or her heart in one pan of a set of scales. In the other pan was a feather. If there was imbalance, if the heart of the deceased weighed more than the feather, he or she was denied admittance to the afterworld. Only the lighthearted were deemed advanced enough to merit immortality.

Now, in a culture such as ours, where the tyranny of the dull mind holds sway, we can expect our intelligentsia to write off Egyptian heart-weighing as quaint superstition, to dismiss squirrel-chatter illumination as flaky Asian guru woo woo. Fine. But what about the Euro-American Trickster tradition, what about Coyote and Raven and Loki and Hermes and the community-sanctioned blasphemies of the clown princes of Saturnalia? For that matter, what about Dada, Duchamp, and the 'pataphysics of Alfred Jarry? What about *Gargantua* and *Finnegans Wake,* John Cage and Erik Satie, Gurdjieff and Robert Anton Wilson, Frank Zappa and Antoni Gaudí? What about Carlos Castaneda, Picasso, and the alchemists of Prague? Allen Ginsberg and R. D. Laing, Rahsaan Roland Kirk and Lewis Carroll, Alexander Calder and Italo Calvino, Henry Miller, Pippi Longstocking, Andrei Codrescu, Ishmael Reed, Alan Rudolph, Mark Twain, and the electric Kool-Aid acid pranksters? What about the sly tongue-in-cheek subversions of Nietzsche (yes, Nietzsche!), and what about Shakespeare, for God's sake, the mega-bard in whose plays, tragedies included, three thousand puns, some of them real groaners, have been verifiably cataloged?

Obviously, while crazy wisdom may have been better appreciated in Asia, nuggets of meaningful playfulness have long twinkled here and there in the heavy iron crown of western tradition. (It was a Spanish poet, Juan Ramón Jiménez, who advised, "If they give you ruled paper, write the other way.") The question is, when will we be hip enough (thank you, Fred) to realize that these sparklers aren't mere rhinestones or baubles of paste? When will our literati – in many cases an erudite, superbly talented lot – evolve to the degree that they accord buoyancy and mirth a dime's worth of the respect they bestow so lavishly on gravity and misfortune?

Norman N. Holland asked a similar question in *Laughing: A Psychology of Humor,* concluding that comedy is deemed inferior to tragedy primarily because of the social prevalence of narcissistic pathology. In other words, people who are too self-important to laugh at their own frequently ridiculous behavior have a vested interest in gravity because it supports their illusions of grandiosity. According to Professor Donald Kuspit, many people are unable to function without such illusions.

"Capitalism," wrote Kuspit, "encourages the pathologically grandiose self because it encourages the conspicuous consumption of possessions which symbolize one's grandiosity." I would add that rigid, unquestioning allegiance to a particular religious or political affiliation is in much the same way also symptomatic of disease.

Ironically, it's this same malignant narcissism, revealing itself through whining, arrogance, avarice, pique, anxiety, severity, defensive cynicism, and aggressive ambition, that is keeping the vainglorious out of their paradise. Among our egocentric sadsacks, despair is as addictive as heroin and more popular than sex, for the single reason that when one is unhappy one gets to pay a lot of attention to oneself. Misery becomes a kind of emotional masturbation. Taken out on others, depression becomes a weapon. But for those willing to reduce and permeate their ego, to laugh – or meow – it into submission, heaven on earth is a distinct psychological possibility.

III

It's good to bear the preceding in mind when trying to comprehend the indignation with which the East Coast establishment greets work that dares to be both funny and deadly serious in the same breath. The left-handed path runs along terrain upon which the bowtiesattvas find it difficult to tread. Their maps are inaccurate and they have the wrong shoes. So, hi ho, hi ho, it's off to the house of woe they go.

Nobody requires a research fellowship to ascertain that most of the critically lauded fiction of our time concentrates its focus on cancer, divorce, rape, racism, schizophrenia, murder, abandonment, addiction, and abuse. Those things, unfortunately, are rampant in our society and ought to be examined in fiction. Yet, to trot them out in book after book, on page after page, without the transformative magic of humor and imagination – let alone a glimmer of higher consciousness – succeeds only in impeding the advancement of literature and human understanding alike.

Down in Latin America, they also write about bad marriages and ill health (as well as the kind of governmental brutality of which we in the U.S. so far have had only a taste). The big difference, though, is that even when surveying the gritty and mundane aspects of daily life, Latin novelists invoke the dream realm, the spirit realm, the mythic realm, the realm of nature, the inanimate world, and the psychological underworld. In acknowledging that social realism is but one layer of a many-layered cake, in threading the inexplicable and the goofy into their naturalistic narratives, the so-called magic realists not only weave a more expansive, inclusive tapestry but leave the reader with a feverish exaltation rather than the deadening weariness that all too often accompanies the completion of even the most splendidly crafted of *our* books.

Can we really take pride in a literature whose cumulative effect is to send the reader to the bridge with "Good Night, Irene" on his lips?

Freud said that "wit is the denial of suffering." As I interpret it, he wasn't implying that the witty among us deny the *existence* of suffering – all of us suffer to one degree or another – but, rather, that armed with a playful attitude, a comic sensibility, we can deny suffering dominion over our lives, we can refrain from buying shares in the company. Funnel that defiant humor onto the page, add a bracing shot of Zen awareness, and hey, pretty soon life has some justification for imitating art.

Don't misunderstand me: a novel is no more supposed to be a guidebook to universal happiness than a self-indulgent journal of the writer's personal pain. And everyone will agree, I think, that crime is a more fascinating subject than lawful behavior, that dysfunction is more interesting than stability, that a messy divorce is ever so much more titillating than a placid marriage. Without conflict, both fiction and life can be a bore. Should that, however, prohibit the serious author from exploring and even extolling the world's pleasures, wonders, mysteries, and delights?

(Maybe all this neurotic, cynical, crybaby fiction is nothing more than the old classroom dictum, "Write what you know," coming back to haunt us like a chalky ghost. If what you know best is angst, your education commands you not to waste a lot of time trying to create robust characters or describe conditions on the sunny side of the street.)

In any case, the notion that inspired play (even when audacious, offensive, or obscene) enhances rather than diminishes intellectual rigor and spiritual fulfillment; the notion that in the eyes of the gods the tight-lipped hero and the wet-cheeked victim are frequently inferior to the red-nosed clown, such notions are destined to be a hard sell to those who have E. M. Forster on their bedside table and a clump of dried narcissus up their ass. Not to worry. As long as words and ideas exist, there will be a few misfits who will cavort with them in a spirit of *approfondement* – if I may borrow that marvelous French word that translates roughly as "playing easy in the deep" – and in so doing they will occasionally bring to realization Kafka's belief that "a novel should be an ax for the frozen seas around us."

A Tibetan-caliber playfulness may not represent, I'm willing to concede, the only ice ax in the literary toolshed. Should there exist alternatives as available, as effective, as potent, nimble, and refreshing, then by all means hone them and bring them down to the floe. Until I've seen them at work, however, I'll stand by my contention that when it comes to writing, a fusion of prankish Asian wisdom, extra-dimensional Latin magic, and two-fisted North American poetic pizzazz (as exotic as that concept might seem to some) could be our best hope for clearing passageways through our heart-numbing, soul-shrinking, spirit-smothering oceans of frost. We have a gifted, conscientious literati. Wouldn't it be the cat's meow to have an enlightened, exhilarating one, as well?

Harper's, 2004

Till Lunch Do Us Part

From an author's perspective, writing about sex is risky, because if you write well enough, evocatively enough, vividly enough, you make the reader want to put the book aside and go get laid. Writing about food is dangerous for much the same reason, except, of course, that you chance driving your audience to table rather than to bed.

Because it takes more resolve to suddenly flee a theater than to abandon a novel, the filmmaker is largely immune from the danger of over-stimulating captive appetites, although the aftereffect of certain movies can be quite interesting. *Tampopo,* for example, may have been the most conflicting film ever produced for the reason that at its conclusion, at least ninety percent of couples in attendance were surely in an absolute quandary over which to run and do first: feed or fuck.

In my private life, I've endeavored to award a fair, unbiased share of attention to each of the sensual pleasures. In my novels, however, it's a different matter. Risky or not, I've simply been unable to resist the temptation to write about sex, but except for riffs on vegetable stir fry and banana Popsicles in *Half Asleep in Frog Pajamas,* and a well-deserved ode to mayonnaise in *Villa Incognito* (not exactly fare destined to activate the saliva glands of your typical gourmet), I've been willing to leave culinary fiction in the garlic-scented hands of such masters of dinner-plate drama as Jim Harrison and Thomas McGuane. If the pages of my novels are ever damp, it's likely from a substance other than drool.

When, a few years ago, an editor informed me that she was compiling an anthology in which selected celebrities would talk about their most favorite food, I declined to contribute – and not only because I find it impossible to think of myself as a "celebrity" without laughing. I must confess, however, that I seriously considered the topic for a day or two; and recently, after a pal posed the question (he must have been stoned, the wicked fellow), "If you were on death row, what would you request for your last meal?", I gave the subject further attention. I'm thinking about it still . . .

Well, the best thing I ever put in my mouth – no, let me rephrase that – the best *food item* I ever put in my mouth was the foie gras mousse with brown morel sauce that came my lucky way during an alarmingly extravagant lunch at L'Ambroisie, a perennial contender for the heavyweight restaurant championship of Paris. In second place, I'd rank the lamb's tongue vinaigrette at Babbo in New York.

Let me say right here that after having occasionally viewed with suspicion if not disgust those rubbery, grayish-pink, papillae-puckered puds that lie like beached dolphin fetuses in the refrigerated cases of certain butcher shops, I long ago vowed that my lips would never admit entrance to any lingual organ that was not securely anchored inside the oral cavity of a living human female. Yes, but those were beef tongues on display in the shops, and the lamb's tongue vinaigrette was chef Mario Batali's signature dish. How could I be taken seriously by Mario, that jumbo jinn of gastronomy, if I refused to at least sample his favored creation? Now, I'm here to report that in color and texture, lamb's tongue resembles cow's tongue little more than it resembles wagon tongue. Tastewise, the dish proved to be heaven without an asterisk, and I've been wowed by it each of the half-dozen times I've dined at Babbo. But I digress.

Writing about asparagus, as I did briefly in *Fierce Invalids Home From Hot Climates,* was a breeze because I could expound poetically yet accurately on the shape and color of the vegetable, as well as its singularly bloomless place in the otherwise florid lily family. I wisely refrained from so much as mentioning the *taste* of asparagus, because it is virtually impossible to talk about the flavor of one thing without comparing it to the flavor of something else – which is why we're all doomed to hear the cliché "Try it, it tastes like chicken" a thousand times before we die. And with complex dishes such as the two cited above, any lengthy discussion of form and hue would be irrelevant.

So, I've never written about lamb's tongue vinaigrette (layered with mushrooms and topped with a poached egg) or foie gras mousse in brown morel sauce, nor do I intend to do so; and as for requesting one or both of those delicacies for my final repast, let's be serious: the prison warden does not exist who is sympathetic – let alone sophisticated – enough to send off to Paris or Manhattan for lamb's tongue vinaigrette or foie gras mousse in brown morel sauce in order that some condemned rat fink criminal might be catapulted into the Beyond with a purring palate and an ecstatic smile.

No problem. It's no problem because were I planning my death-row menu, neither of the aforementioned haute-cuisine items, as unforgettably toothsome as I know them to be, would sit at the top of my wish list, and they'd be excluded even if money and logistics were no object, and even if I didn't feel guilty about the poor goose and the lamb. The truth is, the food I'd actually prefer for my terminal treat is something more downhome and ordinary – although as last meals go, not entirely traditional. (According to surveys, the exit entrée most often requested by condemned convicts is fried shrimp, which isn't necessarily a terrible choice, except that any shrimp fry available within 30 miles of a maximum-security prison, with the exception of seaside San Quentin, is likely to consist of cocoons of greasy batter swaddling thin, pale, bland crustaceans so long frozen they haven't been near an ocean since Jacques Cousteau was in high school.)

Now I'm an Appalachian boy who grew up on grits and turnip greens, but who, spurred by irrepressible curiosity and a Cancerian stomach rather than any ambitious yearning for upward mobility, later developed an appreciation of fine foods. Certain fare from my childhood still appeals to me, however, and I assure you nostalgia has little or nothing to do with it. Most honest epicures will concede that there exist relatively simple dishes that throughout their lives have banged the oral gong with such proficiency, that have provided such unfailingly consistent pleasure and satisfaction, that, in the end (the literal end), those beloved dishes must be picked ahead of seductive offerings from the celebrated kitchens of Bernard Pacaud or Mario Batali. And that is precisely why I would direct the warden's flunky to fetch to my cell the following items:

A. Salt and pepper.

B. A fresh, squishy loaf of Wonder Bread. (It's rare that I remember a major corporation in my prayers, but lately I've been calling on God to assist the Continental Baking Company in emerging from Chapter 11, worried as I am that that cheery wrapper, with its ebullient red, yellow, and blue balloons, might disappear forever from grocery shelves. Sure, great little bakeries abound [think European earth mother], producing breads chewy, aromatic, dense, and nutritious, but when it comes to the construction of particular sandwiches – tuna-and-kimchee, for example, or crispy Spam – Wonder Bread [think trailer park cheerleader] is indispensable. Who cares if it builds strong bodies twelve ways, eighteen ways, or no way at all? As a support platform – so pliable, so absorbent, so uncomplicated, so sensual, so *ready* – for our most soulful spreads and fillings, Wonder is a natural unnatural wonder.)

C. Two ripe red tomatoes. (Depending on the season and the location of my hypothetical incarceration, this could be a problem. It was with great expectations that I recently attended the Palmetto Tomato Festival near Bradenton, Florida, only to discover that every single tomato on display there was green enough to be mistaken for the Incredible Hulk's left testicle. It's become a national taboo to allow tomatoes to ripen in the fields, and when you see a sign in your supermarket advertising "vine ripe tomatoes," you know you're looking at a lie so blatant it would make the Pentagon blush. To be worthy of its name, a tomato must mature slowly and fully during a very hot, very humid summer. Moreover, as with wine grapes and cigar tobacco, the soil must be chemically perfect. Thanks to global warming, temperatures in the Pacific Northwest are higher these Augusts, yet local tomatoes, even when permitted to ripen in the garden, continue to taste like wet Kleenex; and those grown in hothouses bear the same relationship to an outdoor tomato from Hanover County, Virginia, or truck-farm New Jersey that canned sardines bear to freshly caught salmon. I can only hope that, upon learning of my imminent execution, Good Samaritans in Colorado will be moved to ship me a plump love apple from their backyard patch – and should they happen to be friendly with Hunter S. Thompson, perhaps persuade him to inject it with a little something beforehand. Hunter will know just what I mean, and, trust me, it won't affect the taste of the tomato.)*

---

*When I wrote those lines, Thompson was alive and in bloom. Now, with his sad demise, still more color has faded out of the American scene. Where are the men today whose lives are not beige; where are the writers whose style is not gray?

D. A knife. (Okay, they probably aren't going to let a knife into my death cell: I might accidentally nick myself or else threaten the priest who's come to console me with the spiritual equivalent of "vine ripe tomato" ads. I'll have to cajole a jailer into doing the slicing in his office.)

E. A jar of Best Foods mayonnaise. (Whether it was invented by the personal chef of Duc de Richelieu, or by a gaggle of nymphs entertaining hungry satyrs in an alpine glade, mayonnaise's origins are definitely French, and for that I bow thrice each and every morning in the direction of the Eiffel Tower. My refrigerator contains at present two jars of mayo purchased in France. It also holds jars, squeeze bottles, or tubes of mayonnaise from Spain, Mexico, Germany, Norway, and Poland. There are eight varieties from Japan, including cheese-flavored, corn-flavored, wasabi-flavored, and, the best, Kewpie brand regular. The Japanese have become so smitten with the Western condiment – its texture as silky as a kimono, its tang as understated as the tang of Zen – that today they have a word for a mayonnaise junkie: *mayora*. Order a Domino's pizza in urban Nippon and it will automatically arrive with a mayonnaise topping. You gotta love it! Maybe I should start bowing toward the Tokyo Tower. That notwithstanding, the greatest mayonnaise in the world happens to be . . . America's own Best Foods [or Hellmann's, as it's called east of the Rockies], a claim repeatedly verified in the blind tastings that *mayora* friends and I stage in my kitchen every July. There's nothing the least chauvinistic about it, either: we're capable of pinning a blue ribbon on Al Qaeda mayonnaise if it could cut the mustard. The bottom line is, any halfway evolved human being is going to demand that Best Foods be served at his or her last supper, and those insipid prisoners who'd just as soon eat Miracle Whip probably are deserving of their fate. Pardon refused!)

Now it's obvious, is it not, where this picky procuring has

been leading? Deep inside the steel bowels of a dreary institution somewhere, I'm about to lay out a half-dozen slices of cloud-fluffy, cloud-white Wonder Bread. Then, using my toothbrush or my index finger in lieu of the forbidden knife, I'll lather Best Foods onto all six exposed surfaces, careful to spread the eggy ambrosia from edge to edge, crust to crust, because to do otherwise would dishonor the craft of sandwich-making. Rest assured, fellow connoisseurs, an observer would see me blanket the entire slice and blanket it to a most liberal and generous depth.

You might ask, "Tom, is it safe to try this at home?" Well, I can only report that when I, a lifelong consumer of gargantuan amounts of mayonnaise, underwent an angiographic screening in 1999, the attending physicians said I had the arteries of a twelve-year-old boy. (Of course, they didn't say *which* twelve-year-old boy. I suppose they could have meant that double-wide porker who squirms and farts in the seat in front of you every time you go to a Saturday matinée.)

In any event, once the divine dressing has been plastered to an agreeably hedonistic expanse and depth, I'll step back for a moment and admire the sheen of it, the goopy swooze of it, the innocence and decadence and Brigitte Bardot blondeness of it. Alas, however, the great clock is ticking. I'd better proceed to adding the radiant little circles of tomato (round and red as the lenses in a firebug's spectacles), distributing them sufficiently over three of the heavily mayonnaised planes. That done, I'll sprinkle on a trace of pepper and a lot of salt (remember, I have clear arteries). Finally, I'll lay on the roof slices, and with the heel of my hand, apply just enough pressure so that the ingredients adhere to one another, forming a coherent whole; kind of flattened and splayed and fused; spongy to the touch, restful to the eye, inviting to the bite, secure against any untidy loss of contents.

Voilà! That which you now behold, that at which you

cannot help but cock a gentle snook, are three newborn examples of one of civilized mankind's most unassuming yet wondrous concoctions: the pauper king of lunchland, the naïf whose seemingly primitive genius is sadly undervalued by pucky-wucked canapé-snappers and meat-and-potatoes he-men alike; the modest though ever-spunky ... TOMATO SANDWICH!

A brave little raft in a sea of culinary confusion; the deuce of hearts turned inside out, wild card in the dog-eared deck of summer dining; pot of rubies at the end of a bleached-out rainbow; the tomato sandwich is soft and voluptuous, sweetish and acidic, sunny, accessible, unashamedly fatty, and deceptively sumptuous.

Comfort food, you say? Granted, it *is* comforting although not precisely in that "I-miss-my-mommy" sense that, to some, a bowl of good old-fashioned macaroni-and-cheese might be comforting. In fact, few are today's children who would not squawk like a cartoon duck if you plopped a tomato sandwich on their TV tray. No, the properly made tomato sandwich bespeaks a quality beyond adult regression or childish gratification.

For me – and possibly for you as well – there are special foods capable of literally connecting the tastebuds to the soul; foods of which neither my tongue nor my soul ever tires, even were I to eat them every day of my life. And when it comes to tomato sandwiches, I very nearly have.

So, it is completely appropriate that, with a combination of deep reverence and vigorous gusto, I consume a trio of them while awaiting the shadows that are soon to fall across my barred door.

And now here they are, those righteous authorities, all terse and businesslike, scarcely granting me time to wipe my greasy mouth with my sleeve before ushering me out of the cell and down the piss-green corridor to that clean, well-lighted place where I'm to be legally murdered by the state.

Despite having once again enjoyed, in what are scheduled to be my closing minutes, one of life's most agreeable pleasures, I will not falsely claim that I am wholly at peace. Even tomato sandwiches have their limitations. They've left me satiated but, in my current situation, hardly serene. Yet neither am I defiant. And I'm certainly not resigned.

I'm not resigned because, you see, I have a plan. I'm not resigned because this is *my* fantasy, after all, and provided it is dramatically correct, I must insist on a happy ending.

Whoa! What's this? A tremendous explosion has suddenly ripped through the building, throwing me to the floor like a Dear John letter. As debris sifts down upon us, my escorts and I lie there, they stunned, I looking up frantically through the swirling cumulus of dust until I see in the near distance the beckoning lights of dawn.

Bleeding, soiled, lame, I hop through the rubble on one leg, like a flamingo in a sack race. With surprising speed, I'm out into the exercise yard. The guard tower has toppled and in the prison wall there's a hole so wide you could fit an hour's worth of corporate greed in it and have room left over for all of Dick Cheney's draft deferments. Wow! My friends in the Mad Scientists Underground sure know how to orchestrate a jailbreak!

In the deserted street outside the prison walls, Naomi Watts waits in a black Ferrari, its engine revving like a velvet chainsaw. I get in, give Naomi a kiss, she pops the clutch, and off we rocket, barreling down to Mexico at 110 miles an hour. Mexico. Our good neighbor to the south. Mexico, where nowadays sliced bread is widely available, where the lime-flavored mayonnaise is *muy bueno,* and where the tomatoes – if not harvested prematurely or shampooed in pesticide – are *muy* damn *bueno,* indeed.

What Is Art and If We Know What Art Is, What Is Politics?

"Whoever communicates to his brothers in suffering the secret splendor of his dreams acts upon the surrounding society like a solvent, and makes all who understand him, often without their realization, outlaws and rebels."

– Pierre Quillard

The most useful thing about art is its uselessness.

Have I lost you already? Wait a minute. My point is that there's a place – an important place, as a matter of fact – in our all too pragmatic world for the impractical and the non-essential, and that art occupies that place more gloriously than does just about anything else; occupies it with such authority and with such inspirational if quixotic results that we find ourselves in the contradictory position of having to concede that the non-essential can be very essential, indeed, if for no other reason than that an environment reduced to essentials is a subhuman environment in which only drones will thrive.

Taking it a step further, perhaps, let's proclaim that art has no greater enemy than those artists who permit their art to become subservient to socio-political issues or ideals. In so doing, they not only violate art's fundamental sovereignty, they surrender that independence from function that made it art (as opposed to craft or propaganda) in the first place. At the heart of any genuine aesthetic response are sensations that have no rational application, material or psychological, yet somehow manage to enrich our lives.

The notion that art must be an instrument for discernible social betterment is Calvinistic, and the work that is guided by that premise is fundamentally puritanical, even when its content is sexually explicit.

Obviously, art doesn't exist in a vacuum. Like a coral animal, it is embedded in a vast undulating reef of economics, politics, religion, entertainment, and social movements of one kind or another. Yet, while we are in art's thrall, we're lifted out of mundane context and granted a temporary visa to a less ordinary dimension, where our existential burden is momentarily lifted and we surf a wave of pure perceptual pleasure. And what is art, after all, but a vehicle for the transportation of perceptual (i.e. aesthetic) values?

This is not to say that a work of art can't convey other, additional values, values with intellectual and/or emotional heft. However, if it's really art, then those values will play a secondary role. To be sure, we may praise a piece for its cultural insights, for the progressive statement it makes and the courageous stand it takes, but to honor it as "art" when its aesthetic impact is not its dominant feature is to fall into a philistine trap of shoddy semantics and false emphasis.

Speaking of semantics, let's pause for an irritating second or two and define our terms. Ask most people what the word "aesthetic" means and they'll unhesitantly answer, "beauty." Sorry, friends, it just ain't so. Beauty is frequently the major generative force in aesthetics, for the artist and his or her audience alike – but beauty isn't a necessary ingredient in an aesthetic enterprise nor does it by any means define one. In aesthetics, beauty and ugliness are relative terms, and whether a piece is one or the other is often merely a matter of taste.

Like ethics, logic, theology, epistemology, metaphysics, etc., aesthetics is a branch of philosophy, in this case the branch that deals with our powers of sensory perception; more specifically, with how we attempt to understand and evaluate the external phenomena registered by our eyes and ears. When the composition that delights, thrills, captivates, or challenges our sensory receptors has been created for that very purpose, we call it *art*.

Artistic creation is a mysterious venture about which little can be said that isn't misleading. To attempt to pin down art, to lock it in the airless closet of tight definition is boorish, even totalitarian. Yet unless we have somewhat of a consensus about what art is, unless we can evaluate it within certain aesthetic parameters, however flexible and broad, we cannot claim it as a subject. In the latter part of the twentieth century, it became hip to assert, "Hey, man, *everything* is art." That convenient notion is as evasive as it is inclusive, for if everything is art, then hey, man, *nothing* is art. If there's no separate category of human production that can be identified as "art," then we can no longer discuss art, let alone isolate it in a coherent exhibition or hold it to standards of excellence; art will have become indistinguishable from the manufactured flotsam and jetsam under whose weight the crust of the earth (and likely the collective soul) is slowly cracking, sinking, festering.

* * * * * * * * * * *

Politics, too, is a somewhat nebulous subject. It has been defined as "the art (sic) of compromise," ignoring the fact that artists historically have been among the least compromising of individuals, or that while most universities offer degrees in political *science,* none to my knowledge teach political *art.*

Personally, I define politics as "the ambition to preside over property and make other people's decisions for them." Politics, in other words, is an organized, publicly sanctioned amplification of the infantile itch to always have one's own way.

But let's not eat off the cynic's plate. Certainly, ninety percent of the planet's politicians have a single unwavering goal: to gain power, hold on to it at all costs, and reap the rewards. Yet there is political thought and political action that is altruistic and humanistic, free of narcissism and avarice (temporarily, at least: the truest of all truisms is the one that declares that sooner or later power corrupts). There are political agendas that champion pacifism, civil rights, health care, and environmental preservation, and those agendas merit our support and respect. What they do *not* merit is an uncontested usurpation of our art.

Socio-political statements, however laudable, however crucial, can cause the less sophisticated viewer to overlook the fact that the art delivering those statements is often inept, derivative, and trite. When we accept bad art because it's good politics, we're killing the swan to feed the chickens.

Those who would refute my contention that art and politics run on parallel tracks and seldom the twain shall meet inevitably confront me with the example of Picasso's *Guernica*. There's no denying that that monumental 1937 masterpiece was a direct result of Picasso's revulsion at the unprecedented saturation bombing of a civilian village (a common military tactic nowadays, sad to say), or that the painting was intended as an impassioned protest against war in general (war being the all–too–frequent terminus of the political trajectory). However, had Picasso allowed his stirred feelings to override his radical painterly principles, had he produced a traditional, literal, unimaginative rendering of military atrocity instead of this wild, virtuoso outpouring of Cubistic invention, you can bet the ranch dressing that now,

TOM ROBBINS

70 years later, museum visitors would not be standing before it in awe.

What moves us finally in *Guernica* are the surprising range of its monochromatic colors, its dynamic lines, disturbing anatomical dislocations, bizarre metamorphoses, shocking fragmentations, and those raw, mysterious symbols that resonate with such potency in our psyches, even though they may never be completely understood by our rational minds.

Guernica succeeds politically because it first and foremost succeeds aesthetically. The memories it may once have invoked of Spanish fascism have long ago been eclipsed by the explosive, exhilarating force with which it deconstructs form and distributes it about the picture plane. Despite its underpinnings of horror and outrage, it is primarily a visual experience.

Because of the way they say "yes" to life – and thus automatically say "no" to those ideas and actions that threaten life or restrict it – there's a sense in which Renoir's rosy nudes, Calder's dancing amoebas, and Warhol's deadpan soup cans (to pick just three examples) are as much a condemnation of brutality as Picasso's *Guernica*. Interpreted as antiwar statements, are they not then political? Seen from that angle, they are. But in the works of Renoir, Calder, and Warhol, even more than in *Guernica,* the political implications are subtle, ambiguous, and, most important, subordinate to the aesthetic. That's what makes them art.

And art, like love, is what makes the world forever fresh and new. However, this revitalization cannot be said to be art's purpose. Art revitalizes precisely because it *has* no purpose. Except to engage our senses. The emancipating jounce of inspired uselessness.

Morris Louis: Empty and Full

One of the more pleasant paradoxes of McLuhanization is that a "bush-league" town like Seattle can nurture a sensibility enlightened enough to organize, catalog, and mount a major exhibition of Morris Louis while at the same time – by virtue of the provincialism which persists here in spite of the new global togetherness – can afford an opportunity to view Louis in fresh context.

Sensibly, Seattle's Contemporary Art Council resisted the impulse to attempt a Louis retrospective. It chose, instead, to restrict itself to two periods – the so-called "veils" and "unfurleds" – of the artist's career, a decision that was not only realistic but one which permitted a more studied appreciation of the prowess of Louis's talent than would have a less concentrated sampling of all four of his major periods. For one thing, there is greater stylistic variety within the veil series and the unfurled series than may be found within the paintings known as "florals" or those known as "stripes." Moreover, the pairing of veils and unfurleds illustrated dramatically the dazzling creative leaps of which Louis was capable – the veils and unfurleds are virtually pictorial *opposites*.

In the veils, airy Niagaras of integrated color configurations flood their large supports from framing-edge to framing-edge; in the unfurleds, individual irregular ribbons of opaque color are stacked at the sides of equally large canvases, leaving in the interiors vast expanses of surface of approximately the same size and shape as the veil image – but *blank*.

Finally, since the specificity of its ambition allowed it to stress quality rather than quantity – of the 22 enormous pictures in the exhibition, at least 15 represent Louis at the summit of his achievement – the council was able to borrow from the Louis estate several important works which never had been displayed before.

Among the previously unexhibited pictures was *Tau,* a significant variant on the unfurled theme. *Tau* can be read as a greatly enlarged detail from one of the banked ribbon configurations of a more typical unfurled. Magnified, the ribbons (or rivulets) – flowing diagonally from framing-edge to framing-edge (and, by implication, indefinitely beyond) – take on an ominousness of shape that is only partly relieved by the resounding brilliance of their colors. In these proportions, the ribbons of consistent color become even more difficult to read as drawing than when of "normal" size; indeed, any relationship with a human creator is nearly impossible for the eye to establish.

Tau, to my knowledge, is the only picture in which Louis's romanticism seems more sardonic than benign: the proximity of large individual shapes manufactures a visual field that is oppressive, whereas Louis's picture planes usually are almost seductively inviting.

Overhang, another variant, appears to be a transitional painting that successfully bridges the veil and floral periods. The color configurations are more distinct, more tangible than in the usual veil, but they are monadelphous to the extent that they resist establishing planes or Cubistic juxtapositions, a condition that, as Michael Fried has pointed out, created problems in some of the florals.

The Seattle exhibition made possible a consideration of

Louis not usually afforded. The Seattle art community is neither ignorant of the perspicuous formal analyses of Louis made by Greenberg and Fried, nor are we naïve enough to believe that in modernistic painting content can exist independently of form. We are, however, at sufficient distance from the citadels of formalist criticism that we may – with comfort – allot more than the usual priority to the experiential aspects of Louis's work. That Louis was a visionary painter is beyond question. But if he ever spoke of the nature of his philosophical predilections, his friends have been notably reticent on the subject. We might, however, consider several ways in which Louis's work regularly transcends its own materiality – and even its predominant opticality – to provide experiences which can probably best be described as metaphysical.

Along with certain paintings by Pollock, Rothko, Reinhardt, and Robert Irwin, Louis's veils and unfurleds project an "extraterrestrial" presence as opposed to the "sea-level" character of most art. These descriptions are not as eccentric as they would at first appear.

At sea level, weight and gravity are, for all practical purposes, interchangeable. Likewise, in most painting, weight (a condition of pictorial density usually prescribed by opulence of pigment, fullness of volume, or darkness of value) is also inseparable from gravity (a condition of pictorial force usually prescribed by changes of rhythm, dynamics of contour, or balance of plane – in short, those elements which exert tension upon the picture plane and within the eye of the beholder). In outer space, however, weight and gravity can, and normally do, occur independently of one another.

From a height of 200 miles, the gravity field in which an astronaut is moving still has ninety percent of its terrestrial value, yet his weight is exactly nothing. The undulation of rivulets in the unfurleds and the lucid interchanges of color configurations in the veils exert a relatively profound gravitational force from which the eye of the observer is never free, yet despite Louis's scale – partly because of it – the atmospheric posture and subtle balance of tensions in these pictures is such that they seem absolutely *weightless*.

Before the veils and unfurleds, the observer experiences the exhilaration man almost always feels when he succeeds in soaring free from the earth – an exhilaration that is particularly sensational but which evokes conditions of consciousness that are essentially spiritual. It is no coincidence that the gods of so many disparate cultures have dwelt in the sky.

Space in the veils and unfurleds embodies an act of manipulation with obvious supra-optic overtones. In the unfurleds, Louis *parted* the veils – he removed the huge continuous image which had obscured, however transparently, the center of his canvases. The space subsequently exposed, although blank, proved surprisingly to be neither dull nor dead. It possessed not only color and shape but a spatial presence at least as strong as that of the veils. Such a phenomenon could be analogous to numerous references in mystic literature to the very real substance of that formlessness which exists when form has gone.

Too, from a certain perspective the unfurleds' banks of ribbons look to be waves or beams which have been deflected by an area of space of such substance that it is impenetrable. From another perspective the same ribbons seem to be floating like banners in a space that is entirely vaporous.

In either case, a sense of the *void* is conveyed with a reality unequaled in all of art. And, as in most Eastern philosophies, it is a void simultaneously full and empty, nothing and everything.

ARTFORUM, September 1967

Lost in Translation

Those Americans familiar with my work (don't everybody stand up at once) will not be surprised to learn that one of the questions I'm asked most frequently is, "How do your books come across in foreign translations?"

Well, for readers who are interested in such matters, there's probably no better answer than the following example.

First, here are some opening paragraphs from the prologue to my 1984 novel, *Jitterbug Perfume.*

The beet is the most intense of vegetables. The radish, admittedly, is more feverish, but the fire of the radish is a cold fire, the fire of discontent not of passion. Tomatoes are lusty enough, yet there runs through tomatoes an undercurrent of frivolity. Beets are deadly serious.

Slavic peoples get their physical characteristics from potatoes, their smoldering inquietude from radishes, their seriousness from beets.

The beet is the melancholy vegetable, the one most willing to suffer. You can't squeeze blood out of a *turnip* ...

The beet is the murderer returned to the scene of the crime. The beet is what happens when the cherry finishes with the carrot. The beet is the ancient ancestor of the autumn moon, bearded, buried, all but fossilized; the dark green sail of the grounded moon-boat stitched with veins of primordial plasma; the kite string that once connected the moon to the Earth now a muddy whisker drilling desperately for rubies.

Now, here is a literal back-translation into English of those same sentences as they appear in a version published in the Czech Republic.

Among all vegetables, the red beet is the most passionate. The radish may be hotter, but her heat soars in the cold flame of anxiety, not passion. Tomatoes may be sufficiently energetic, but then, they are known for their carelessness. The beet is mortally serious.

The Slavic nations developed their body characteristics thanks to the potatoes, their smoldering restlessness from radishes, and the seriousness from the red beet.

The red beet is a melancholy vegetable, always prepared to suffer. And from such turnip you can not get any blood . . .

The red beet is a murderer who keeps returning to the place of the crime. The red beet predicts what is going to happen when a cherry knocks off the carrot. The red beet is an ancient ancestor of the harvest moon, with beard, buried and fully petrified; of the dark green sails on the lunar boat stitched with elementary plasma; of the kite line which once tied together the Earth and the Moon, to be changed at the end into muddy whisker frantically searching for rubies.

The reader can now draw his or her own conclusions. Obviously, though, some translations are more precise than others. I've been told by bilingual readers that until recently, when the insensitive publisher unduly hurried the translator, I've been reproduced in Italian with scant loss of meaning or intent; but that the Mexican Spanish version of *Even Cowgirls Get the Blues* is quite "sleazy," a description that probably doesn't displease me as much as it ought.

Incidentally, *Jitterbug Perfume* in Czech back-translates into *Perfume of the Insane Dance*. I'm not sure that I don't prefer that title to my own. So, if much is lost in translation, something on rare occasions may also be gained.

Leo Kenney and the Geometry
of Dreaming

What we have here is a thirty-year record of one man's search for the Self through art.

It is that poignant and that personal. And because it is an adventure of the imagination, because for Leo Kenney the process of making visible connections between himself and the rest of the universe has been so very nearly ceremony or rite, because at its best his work does not even have the look of Art, the temptation is strong (especially at this flaccid moment in our cultural history) to deal with the Kenney exhibition in metaphysical rather than aesthetic terms.

Happily, however, the formal aspects of Kenney's painting match the measure of his psychological/philosophical quest. If his meditations on mysterious relationships encompass the physical act of applying pigment to paper and, indeed, overtake it, it is still all there before our eyes, all of it, externalized and none the weaker after hard-nosed analysis. The human imagination has always searched for abstract symbols with which to express itself. We need extend our evaluation of Kenney no further than the actual formal means by which he has manifested that search in order to reach a full experiential appreciation of the visionary phenomena that have informed and intuited it.

First, let us divide Kenney's lifework thus far into two bodies: that done prior to 1962 and that executed thereafter. Actually, of course, there are several "periods" represented by the sixty-eight works in this retrospective, but, taking a broad view, it is evident that a sharp stylistic demarcation occurred around 1962, when the artist was thirty-seven, was back at art after a fairly long absence, and was contemplating a return to his native Pacific Northwest from California. Freud stresses in his investigations the passages and difficulties of the first half of the human life cycle – those of our infancy and adolescence. Jung, on the other hand, has emphasized the crises of the second half – when, in order to advance, the sun of our being must submit to setting. Thus, at the risk of oversimplification, we might say that before 1962, Leo Kenney was a Freudian painter, after 1962, Jungian.

These categories sound less arbitrary when we note that the "Freudian" paintings are decidedly flavored with Surrealism, their subject matter and optical placements a testimony to that teeming, Freud-discovered substratum of consciousness wherein the distinction between the sensory and the intellectual functioning of the mind is erased. The pictures that we shall call "Jungian" employ a much more clarified, accessible, and universal set of symbols, presented in an oceanic atmosphere of radiance and calm.

Speaking of subject matter, the "Freudian" paintings contain an abundance of it. This is figurative work, on both a literal and symbolic level. The central configuration in *The Inception of Magic,* the earliest work (1945) in the show, is a human torso, complete with distended womb, through which flow all manner of physical and psychic forces, and which is composed of an orchestrated synthesis of macrocosmic and microcosmic imagery. As late as 1961, in *Relic of the Sun,* this same torso is dealt with again, although now the emphasis is on volume rather than on line, on archetypal shape rather than on internal energies.

The representational figures and objects of the "Freudian" period are quite linear. Frequently, Kenney combined ink drawing with water-soluble paints (although there are several fine oils in this show, Kenney is by inclination and reputation a watercolorist and that is how we shall regard him). His line here is precise, intense, as architectural as organic but absolutely throbbing with sensuality. His color is subdued and subordinate, often no more than a tonal exercise in grays.

These works are literary to the point of being *reading* rather than visual experiences. Hermetic, romantic, incredibly introspective, they are packed edge to edge with images-within-images, heads dreaming other heads, emotions and thoughts stylized into symbols – in short, they are overloaded with the cerebral speculations, philosophical yearnings, and erotic anxieties of a brilliant young provincial who had rejected all formal education and then proceeded to drink himself giddy on art books, Surrealist and Symbolist poetry, West Coast art museum collections, and the ceremonial trappings of the Catholic Church, which he attended until his early teens.

Today, such painting is hardly fashionable, and Kenney's "Freudian" pictures may seem stilted and theatrical. They are, also, extremely moving. Moreover, the loving, even obsessive, attention that he lavished on his enigmatic juxtapositions, his quasi-Renaissance perspectives, his hallucinatory unfoldings and planar undulations often produced pictures of real beauty. In *Night Swimmer II,* for example, the timing of the various pictorial elements is so exquisite as to transport the viewer beyond considerations of iconography.

Kenney's "Freudian" paintings – and *in distillation,* the later work, too – have an affinity with, if not a debt to, Giorgio de Chirico, Henry Moore, Max Ernst, and the Salvador Dali of the *Soft Construction With Boiled Beans* persuasion; with Neo-Romanticism and perhaps even Synthetic Cubism. It is best to place him in that sort of international context. While his presence on the doorsteps of Mark Tobey, Guy Anderson, and, especially, Morris Graves was a source of strength and inspiration for him, and while he shares a few of those artists' general characteristics, it is misleading to see Kenney as a younger but bona fide member of a so-called "Northwest School." He creates from an intuitive and individual imperative, with ties to many eras and areas of art.

It is no labor to find evolutionary continuity in Kenney's work. The forms from the early pictures are echoed in the later, and the artist maintains his philosophical proclivities. But, following a deeply mystical personal experience in 1962, a purification took place. The "Freudian" paintings were stripped of extraneous and overtly figurative imagery; concerns were clarified, simplified, abstracted, and placed in the mainstream of the collective unconscious. In the "Jungian" works, Kenney employs a few simple, ancient geometric devices in variation – most often the circle and the square in that order.

Of all emblems, the circle or "tondo" is the most soaked with meaning. From dimmest pre-history, it has symbolized the sun, whose power, in one disguise or another, flows through all matter. It represents, too, the seed and the cell, the head, the halo and the corona, bodily orifices, Zodiac wheels, the earth, the eye, and the egg, the unbroken cycle of life and the continuity of consciousness. In Kenney's hands it alludes unspecifically to all these things, as well as to what Tibetans call the "mysterious golden flower of the soul." Kenney's tondos are magic mirrors that objectify subjectives.

Formally, he puts the circle to more pragmatic uses. Its round shape serves to draw the viewer's eye inward toward a nucleus where it is confronted either by a more finite system of circles that suggest the viewer must look deeper still, or by spikes, sparks, or effluvia, that especially when deployed concentrically, also push pictorial space *outward*, heightening the illusion of spatial vastness and placing the internal forms in a more communicative relationship with the framing edges.

The square, too, has symbolic overtones. Early Chinese used it to represent the world. It also has been glorified as a sacred portal, and its four corners have served as visual metaphors for air, earth, fire, and water. To Kenney, the square functions chiefly as a container. It limits and directs the emanations of the circles (thereby playing the dominant, or male, role to the circle's passive, or female, role). It also helps to balance Kenney's compositions, allowing them to be read, on one level, as studies in symmetry. The plastic dialogue between squares and circles (and occasional rectangles and ellipsoids) is responsible for the dynamic theater of tensions which dominates everything in Kenney's pictures, even the symmetry.

This pictorial drama reflects an actual drama that is unfolding somewhere "out there" or "in here," but the nature of the drama cannot be specifically identified. It is either too macrocosmic or too microcosmic for the mind's eye to bring completely into focus. Kenney is a purveyor of ambiguities, paradoxes, and dualities – all in the service of giving geometric form to the mysterious relationships that exist between everything in the cosmos.

Simultaneously, with the beginning of the "Jungian" period, we have the emergence of Kenney as a masterful and innovative colorist. And the surprise, here, is that while his forms have become more universal, his blossoming palette is uniquely personal.

Neither organic nor synthetic, his colors come entirely from his imagination. While some of our best contemporary painters force us into an encounter with pure color, Kenney's color seduces us into an encounter with Kenney. Instead of optical dazzle, he offers us subjective illuminations. Although his use of color is far from primitive, it seems innocent and true.

Kenney is a tonal painter. In any one picture, you may find an economy of colors but an extravagance of tones. In a subtle and harmonious way, these tones modify, inflect, inspire, and cancel each other to the point where we do not readily distinguish individual generic colors but rather experience a vast aura of tones in constant, orchestral modulation of each other. This is true even though there frequently are large areas to which only a single tone has been applied. Kenney's "total color" effect is, therefore, not so much the result of a profusion of closely juxtaposed values as it is the result of a carefully controlled overall *radiance*. His colors intermingle in the way that gases do; they interact as vapor interacts with light.

Kenney's primary medium is gouache, a water-soluble pigment which he applies to dampened paper. This technique gives a soft, spreading, almost blurry effect but one which is nonetheless opaque. Such interchangeability of surface qualities – on the one hand translucent and evanescent, on the other, absorbent and dense – creates an illusion of both concreteness and great depth. And despite the softness of the medium, Kenney's range is such that he can intensify colors to the point where they seem fluorescent.

Observe these paradoxes: Kenney's color is soft yet intense; his color is cool yet it glows as if afire; it is water-based yet it is alkaline dry; it is rigorous yet it is highly sensual and sometimes very nearly sweet.

While he can – and does – use greens, browns, and yellows, Kenney's favored hues are reds and blues. What kind of reds and blues? Mixtures of amaranth and orchid, grape and starfish, electricity and high blood pressure. They are like hues perceived through telescopes or microscopes; the colors of sunspots, novae, ionized auroras, and Saturnian rings; of arteries, nerve filaments, viruses, and reproductive cells. In their ambiguity, Kenney's colors are both intimate and alien. They inspire unconscious connections between entities as close as our own vital organs and as distant as the farthest stars.

* * * * * * * * * * *

This retrospective is far from a finalized statement. At forty-eight, Kenney is alive and well – and hinting at new directions. Consider *Lake Gemma,* a recent work. In it, the artist turns his attentions to the parallelogram and the effect is as if Josef Albers had emerged, at long last, from the dusty drafting rooms of the Bauhaus to be suddenly bowled over by nocturnal raptures: the quadrilateral becomes poetically charged, bearing witness to the interdependence of spirit and matter, in nature and art. And bearing witness to Kenney's visual resourcefulness as he persists in his search for Self, which is to say, for higher consciousness.

Painting for Kenney is part of a total life-process. He lives and he paints as freely as possible, resisting any impulse to categorize or solidify. He rarely begins a picture with an idea in mind; rather, when his psychological stirrings become particularly acute, he knows it is time to involve himself in the physical art of applying paint to paper. In contrast to the intellectualized painting that is dominant today, Kenney's method is almost a ritual – an acting out of mysterious desires, a crystallization of vague urges, a channeling of shadows through a Euclidean grid.

Plato is reported to have said, "God geometrizes." It would be difficult to name another mortal artist today who puts geometry to such divine purposes as does Leo Kenney – and makes it count on the picture plane.

Seattle Art Museum, 1973

The Desire of His Object

In a society that is essentially designed to organize, direct, and gratify mass impulses, what is there to minister to the silent zones of man as an individual? Religion? Art? Nature? No, the church has turned religion into standardized public spectacle, and the museum has done the same for art. The Grand Canyon and Niagara Falls have been looked at so much that they've become effete, sucked empty by too many insensitive eyes. What is there to minister to the silent zones of man as an individual? Well, how about a cold chicken bone on a paper plate at midnight, how about a lurid lipstick lengthening or shortening at your command, how about a styrofoam nest abandoned by a "bird" you've never known, how about whitewashed horseshoes crucified like lucky iron Jesuses above a lonely cabin door, how about something beneath a seat touched by your shoe at the movies, how about worn pencils, cute forks, fat little radios, boxes of bow ties, and bubbles on the side of a bathtub? Yes, these are the things, these kite strings and olive oil cans and velvet hearts stuffed with pubic hair, that form the bond between the autistic psyche and the experiential world; it is to show these things in their true mysterious light that is the purpose of the moon.

– Still Life With Woodpecker (1980)

Whether Ken Cory ever read the preceding lines, or if so, whether he completely agreed with them, we cannot know. It is certain, however, that he would have understood them. The relationship between humanity and so-called lifeless objects is often more complex and enigmatic than the connection between humanity and nature. In the shifting psychological shadows of the organic/inorganic trellis, Cory tended his grapes and pressed his wine.

Many of us feel trapped, oppressed, compromised by the excess of material goods that surround and sometimes beleaguer us. Yet, despite our expressed intention to simplify our existence, we continue to amass objects of all uses and sizes – to save us time, bolster our status, extend our egos, or insulate us falsely against the approaching December of death. The possibility that the things themselves might possess a personality, an energy, a matrix of meaning beyond the pragmatic, beyond the symbolic, beyond the totemic, beyond the aesthetic, even, is a notion that normally eludes us. Apparently, it did not elude Ken Cory.

If art deals with the philosophy of life, and craft with the philosophy of materials, Cory – like one of those sweet pink dumb phallic erasers he admired – scuffed out the line between the two (much as, on a more specific level, he blurred the boundary between elegance and funk).

His ornaments have been called "tiny sculptures," but that seems not quite exact. They are too theatrical, too narrative, to fit any formalist definition of sculpture. More accurately, they are tiny tableaus. A Cory creation may function as a pin, an ashtray, or a buckle, but what he has actually produced is a miniature environment. He constructed little worlds. And in those small worlds he made his secret home.

If the objects and images he so meticulously fashioned and fervently collected reflect his personal proclivities, they also, simultaneously, reveal the hidden character of the things themselves. In other words, Cory did not merely endow his pieces with humor, bawdiness, poetry, vitality, beauty, and mystery, he had the vision to recognize that those qualities were implicit in the "objective" materials all along.

Like the ancients, Ken Cory moved in a divinely animated universe – animated even when it was static and mute, divine even when it was goofy and crass.

Drawn to junkyards, garage sales, and hardware stores the way a mystic is drawn to a mountaintop, a satyr to a rutting ground, or a beekeeper to a hive, Cory clearly *needed* the theater of objecthood. Perhaps it needed him, as well.

Tacoma Art Museum, 1997

RESPONSES

Write About One of
Your Favorite Things

To pragmatists, the letter Z is nothing more than a phoneti-cally symbolic glyph, a minor sign easily learned, readily assimilated, and occasionally deployed in the course of a lit-erate life. To cynics, Z is just an S with a stick up its butt.

Well, true enough, any word worth repeating is greater than the sum of its parts; and the particular word-part Z – angular, whereas S is curvaceous – can, from a certain perspective, appear anally wired (although Z is far too sophisticated to throw up its arms like Y and act as if it had just been goosed).

On those of us neither prosaic nor jaded, however, those whom the Fates have chosen to monitor such things, Z has had an impact above and beyond its signifying function. A presence in its own right, it's the most distant and elusive of our twenty-six linguistic atoms; a mysterious, dark figure in an otherwise fairly innocuous lineup, and the sleekest little swimmer ever to take laps in a bowl of alphabet soup.

Scarcely a day of my life has gone by when I've not stirred the alphabetical ant nest, yet every time I type or pen the letter Z, I still feel a secret tingle, a tiny thrill. This is partially due to Z's relative rarity: my dictionary devotes 99 pages to A words, 138 pages to P, but only 5 pages to words beginning with Z. Then there's Z's exoticness, for, though it's a component of the English language, it gives the impression of having zipped out of Africa or the ancient Near East of Nebuchadnezzar. Ultimately, perhaps, what is most fascinating about Z is its dual projection of subtle menace and aesthetic grace. Zs are not verbal ants; they are bees. Stylish bees. Killer bees. They buzz; they sting.

Z is a whip crack of a letter, a striking viper of a letter, an open jackknife ever ready to cut the cords of convention or peel the peach of lust.

A Z is slick, quick (it's no accident that automakers call their fastest models Z cars), arcane, eccentric, and always faintly sinister – although its very elegance separates it from the brutish X, that character traditionally associated with all forms of extinction. If X wields a tire iron, Z packs a laser gun. Zap! If X is Mike Hammer, Z is James Bond. (For reasons known only to the British, a Z 007 would pronounce its name "zed.") If X marks the spot, Z *avoids* the spot, being too fluid, too cosmopolitan, to remain in one place.

In contrast to that prim, trim, self-absorbed supermodel, I, or to O, the voluptuous, orgasmic, bighearted slut, were Z a woman, she would be a femme fatale, the consonant we love to fear and fear to love.

The celebrities of the alphabet are M and Z, the letters for whom famous movies have been named. Of course, V had its novel, but as I can assure you from personal experience, in today's culture a novel lacks a movie's sizzle, not to mention pizzazz. Is it not testimony to Z's star power that it is invariably selected to come on last – and this despite the fact that the F word gets all the press?

Take a letter? You bet. I'll take Z. My favorite country, at least on paper, is Zanzibar; my favorite body of water, the Zuider Zee. ZZ Top is my favorite band, zymology my favorite branch of science (dealing, as it does, with the fermentation of beverages).

Had Zsa Zsa Gabor married Frank Zappa, she would have had the coolest name in the world – except, maybe, if ZaSu Pitts had wed Tristan Tzara. As for me, my given name, Thomas, is a modern, anglicized version of the old prebiblical moniker Tammuz. Originally, Tammuz was a mythological hero who served the Goddess simultaneously as lover, husband, brother, and son. Give me my Z back, and there's no telling where I might go from there.

Before I go *anywhere*, however, let me lift a zarf of zinfandel to the former ruling family of Russia. To the tzar, the tzarina, and all the little tzardines! And as for those who would complain that I'm taking this bizzness too far, I say: better a zedophile than a pedophile.

Requested by *Esquire*, 1996

How Do You Feel About America?

America is a nation of 270 million people: 100 million of them are gangsters, another 100 million are hustlers, 50 million are complete lunatics, and every single one of us is secretly in show business. Isn't that fabulous? I mean, how could you fail to have a good time in a country like that? I could live literally anywhere in the world and do what I do, so, obviously, I live in America by choice – not for any patriotic or financial reasons necessarily, but because it's so *interesting* there. America may be the least boring country on earth, and this despite the fact that the dullards on the religious right and the dullards on the academic left (the two faces of yankee puritanism) seem to be in competition to see who can do the most to promote compulsory homogenization and institutionalized mediocrity. It won't work. In America, the chronically wild, persistently haywire, strongly individualistic, surprisingly good-humored, flamboyant con-man hoopla is simply bigger than all of them.

Anthem, Avon Books, 1997

NOTE: The preceding was written several years before the military–industrial complex first seized and then cemented total control of the U.S. government, a coup d'état that would have failed without the active assistance of a rapidly growing population of fearful, non-thinking dupes; "true believers" dumbed down and almost comically manipulated by their media, their church, and their state. So be it. Freedom has long proven too heady an elixir for America's masses, weakened and confused as they are by conflicting commitments to puritanical morality and salacious greed. In the wake of the recent takeover, our prevailing national madness has been ratcheting steadily skyward: the pious semi-literates in the conservative camp tremble and crow, the educated martyrs in the progressive sector writhe and fume. It's a grand show, from a cosmic perspective, though enjoyment of the spectacle is blunted by the havoc being wreaked on nature and by the developmental abuse inflicted on children. We must bear in mind, however, that the central dynamic of our race has never been a conflict between good and evil but rather between enlightenment and ignorance. Ignorance makes the headlines, wins the medals, doles out the punishment, jingles the coin, yet in its clandestine cubbyholes (and occasionally on the public stage) enlightenment continues to quietly sparkle, its radiance outshining the entire disco ball of history. Its day may or may not come, but no matter. The world as it is! Life as it is! Enlightenment is its own reward.

What Do You Think Writer's Block Is and Have You Ever Had It?

I'm not convinced that there's any such thing as "writer's block." I suspect that what we like to call "writer's block" is actually a failure of nerve or a failure of imagination, or both.

If you're willing to take chances, risk ridicule, and push the envelope, and if you've managed to hold on to your imagination (the single most important quality a writer can possess, even slightly more important than an itchy curiosity and a sense of humor), then you can dissolve any so-called block simply by imagining extraordinary, heretofore unthinkable solutions, and/or by playing around uninhibitedly with language. You can imagine or word-play your way out of any impasse. That's assuming, of course, that you're talented in the first place.

Asked by *New Times,* 2002

With What Fictional Character Do You Most Identify?

I'll take Gorodish. And, no, I'm not trying to order the daily special in a Hungarian restaurant. Gorodish happens to be the name of the middle-aged character played by Richard Bohringer in *Diva*, the flashy/spiky 1981 film written and directed by Jean-Jacques Beineix.

Gorodish spends much of each day sitting in a bathtub in the center of his large, virtually empty Parisian loft, smoking cigars and meditating on the undulating blue water in one of those plastic wave machines. He has a teenaged Vietnamese paramour for whom he cares but of whom he is not the least bit possessive; and on the rare occasions when he leaves the loft, he wears handsome white suits and drives a gorgeous vintage white Citroën. As his young friends keep getting into trouble with gangsters, he comes to their aid, swiftly, effectively, and forcefully, but always with faint amusement and the kind of grace that never expends an erg more of energy than is absolutely necessary.

Serenely unattached yet wryly compassionate, Gorodish is coolness personified, the most Zen character in the history of cinema. He's my ideal and, naturally, I want to emulate him, right down to the tub and the cigars – though I know I've got a ways to go. In fact, my own paramour insists that the fictional character I most resemble is not Beineix's Gorodish, but Twain's Tom Sawyer.

Solicited by an editor for inclusion in a survey book not yet published.

Is the Writer Obligated to Use His/Her Medium as an Instrument for Social Betterment?

A writer's first obligation is not to the many-bellied beast but to the many-tongued beast, not to Society but to Language. Everyone has a stake in the husbandry of Society, but Language is the writer's special charge. A grandiose animal it is, too. If it weren't for Language there wouldn't be Society.

Once writers have established their basic commitment to Language (and are taking the Blue-Guitar-sized risks that that relationship demands), then they are free to promote social betterment to the extent that their conscience or neurosis might require. But let me tell you this: social action on the political/economic level is wee potatoes.

Our great human adventure is the evolution of consciousness. We are in this life to enlarge the soul, liberate the spirit, and light up the brain.

How many writers of fiction do you think are committed to *that*?

Asked by *Fiction International*, 1984

Why Do You Live Where You Live?

I'm here for the weather.

Well, yes, I'm also here for the volcanoes and the salmon, and the fascinating possibility that at any moment the volcanoes could erupt and pre-poach the salmon. I'm here for the rust and the mildew, for webbed feet and twin peaks, spotted owls and obscene clams (local men suffer from geoduck envy), blackberries and public art (including that threatening mural the smut-sniffers chased out of Olympia), for the rituals of the potlatch and the espresso cart, for bridges that are always pratfalling into the water and ferries that keep ramming the dock.

I'm here because the Wobblies used to be here, and sometimes in Pioneer Square you can still find bright-eyed old anarchists singing their moldering ballads of camaraderie and revolt. I'm here because someone once called Seattle "the hideout capital of the U.S.A.," a distant outpost of a town where generations of the nation's failed, fed-up, and felonious have come to disappear. Long before Seattle was "America's Athens" *(The New York Times)*, it was America's Timbuktu.

Getting back to music, I'm here because "Tequila" is the unofficial fight song of the University of Washington and because "Louie Louie" very nearly was chosen as our official state anthem. There may yet be a chance of that, which is not something you could say about South Carolina.

I'm here for the forests (what's left of them), for the world's best bookstores and movie theaters; for the informality, anonymity, general lack of hidebound tradition, and the fact that here and nowhere else grunge rubs shoulders in the half-mean streets with a subtle yet pervasive mysticism. The shore of Puget Sound is where electric guitars cut their teeth and old haiku go to die.

I'm here for those wild little mushrooms that broadcast on transcendental frequencies; for Kevin Calabro, who broadcasts Sonics games with erudite exuberance on KJR; for Dick's Deluxe burgers, for the annual Spam-carving contests, the cigar room at Dolce's Latin Bistro, Monday Night Football at the Blue Moon Tavern, opera night at the Blue Moon Tavern (which, incidentally, is scheduled so that it coincides with Monday Night Football – a somewhat challenging overlap that the first-time patron might fail to fully appreciate); and I'm here for the flying saucers that made their first earthly appearance near Mount Rainier.

I'm here for Microsoft but not for Weyerhaeuser. I'm here for Starbucks but not for Boeing. I'm definitely here for the Pike Place Market and definitely not here for Wal-Mart or any scuzzball who shops at Wal-Mart. I'm here for the snow geese in the tide flats but not for the snow jobs in the State House. I'm here for the tulips but not the Tulip Festival (they're flowers, folks, not marketing tools!). I'm here for the relative lack of financial ambition (which, alas, may be responsible for some of those Wal-Mart shoppers), for the soaring population of bald eagles, and the women with their quaint Norwegian brand of lust. "Ya. Sure, ya betcha."

But mostly, finally, ultimately, I'm here for the weather.

As a result of the weather, ours is a landscape in a minor key, a sketchy panorama where objects, both organic and inorganic, lack well-defined edges and tend to melt together, creating a perpetual blurred effect, as if God, after creating Northwestern Washington, had second thoughts and tried unsuccessfully to erase it. Living here is not unlike living inside a classical Chinese painting before the intense wisps of mineral pigment had dried upon the silk – although, depending on the bite in the wind, there're times when it's more akin to being trapped in a bad Chinese restaurant; a dubious joint where gruff waiters slam chopsticks against the horizon, where service is haphazard, noodles soggy, wallpaper a tad too green, and considerable amounts of tea are spilt; but in each and every fortune cookie there's a line of poetry you can never forget. Invariably, the poems comment on the weather.

In the deepest, darkest heart of winter, when the sky resembles bad banana baby food for months on end, and the witch measles that meteorologists call "drizzle" are a chronic gray rash on the skin of the land, folks all around me sink into a dismal funk. Many are depressed, a few actually suicidal. But I, I grow happier with each fresh storm, each thickening of the crinkly stratocumulus. "What's so hot about the sun?" I ask. Sunbeams are a lot like tourists: intruding where they don't belong, promoting noise and forced activity, faking a shallow cheerfulness, dumb little cameras slung around their necks. Raindrops, on the other hand, introverted, feral, buddhistically cool, behave as if they were locals. Which, of course, they are.

My bedroom is separated from the main body of my house, so that I have to go outside and cross some pseudo-Japanese stepping-stones in order to go to sleep at night. Often I get rained on a little bit on my way to bed. It's a benediction, a good-night kiss.

Romantic? Absolutely. And nothing to be ashamed of. If reality is a matter of perspective, then the romantic view of the world is as valid as any other – and a great deal more rewarding. It makes of life an unpredictable adventure rather than a problematic equation. Rain is the natural element for romanticism. A dripping fir is a hundred times more sexy than a sunburnt palm tree, and more primal and contemplative, too. A steady, wind-driven rain composes music for the psyche. It not only nurtures and renews, it consecrates and sanctifies. It whispers in secret languages about the primordial essence of things.

Obviously, then, the Pacific Northwest's customary climate is perfect for a writer. It's cozy and intimate. Reducing temptation (how can you possibly play on the beach or work in the yard?), it turns a person inward, connecting them with what Jung called "the bottom below the bottom," those areas of the deep unconscious into which every serious writer must spelunk. Directly above my writing desk there is a skylight. This is the window, rain-drummed and bough-brushed, through which my Muse arrives, bringing with her the rhythms and cadences of cloud and water, not to mention the latest catalog from Victoria's Secret and the twenty-three auxiliary verbs.

Oddly enough, not every local author shares my proclivity for precipitation. Unaware of the poetry they're missing, many malign the mist as malevolently as the non-literary heliotropes do. They wring their damp mitts and fret about rot, cursing the prolonged spillage, claiming they're too dejected to write, that their feet itch (athlete's foot), the roof leaks, they can't stop coughing, and they feel as if they're being slowly digested by an oyster.

Yet the next sunny day, though it may be weeks away, will trot out such a mountainous array of pagodas, vanilla sundaes, hero chins, and god fingers; such a sunset palette of Jell-O, carrot oil, Vegas strip, and Kool-Aid; such a sea-vista display of broad waters, firred islands, whale spouts, and boat sails thicker than triangles in a geometry book, that any and all memories of dankness will fizz and implode in a blaze of bedazzled amnesia. "Paradise!" you'll hear them proclaim as they call United Van Lines to cancel their move to Arizona.

They're kidding themselves, of course. Our sky can go from lapis to tin in the blink of an eye. Blink again and your latte's diluted. And that's just fine with me. I thrive here on the certainty that no matter how parched my glands, how anhydrous the creek beds, how withered the weeds in the lawn, it's only a matter of time before the rains come home.

The rains will steal down from the Sasquatch slopes. They will rise with the geese from the marshes and sloughs. Rain will fall in sweeps, it will fall in drones, it will fall in cascades of cheap Zen jewelry.

And it will rain a fever. And it will rain a sacrifice. And it will rain sorceries and saturnine eyes of the totem.

Rain will primitivize the cities, slowing every wheel, animating every gutter, diffusing commercial neon into smeary blooms of esoteric calligraphy. Rain will dramatize the countryside, sewing pearls into every web, winding silk around every stump, redrawing the horizon line with a badly frayed brush dipped in tea and quicksilver.

And it will rain an omen. And it will rain a trance. And it will rain a seizure. And it will rain dangers and pale eggs of the beast.

Rain will pour for days unceasing. Flooding will occur. Wells will fill with drowned ants, basements with fossils. Mossy-haired lunatics will roam the dripping peninsulas. Moisture will gleam on the beak of the Raven. Ancient shamans, rained from their rest in dead tree trunks, will clack their clamshell teeth in the submerged doorways of video parlors. Rivers will swell, sloughs will ferment. Vapors will billow from the troll-infested ditches, challenging windshield wipers, disguising intentions and golden arches. Water will stream off eaves and umbrellas. It will take on the colors of the beer signs and headlamps. It will glisten on the claws of nighttime animals.

And it will rain a screaming. And it will rain a rawness. And it will rain a disorder, and hair-raising hisses from the oldest snake in the world.

Rain will hiss on the freeways. It will hiss around the prows of fishing boats. It will hiss in electrical substations, on the tips of lit cigarettes, and in the trash fires of the dispossessed. Legends will wash from the desecrated burial grounds, graffiti will run down alley walls. Rain will eat the old warpaths, spill the huckleberries, cause toadstools to rise like loaves. It will make poets drunk and winos sober, and polish the horns of the slugs.

And it will rain a miracle. And it will rain a comfort. And it will rain a sense of salvation from the philistinic graspings of the world.

Yes, I'm here for the weather. And when I'm lowered at last into a pit of marvelous mud, a pillow of fern and skunk cabbage beneath my skull, I want my epitaph to read, IT RAINED ON HIS PARADE. AND HE WAS GLAD!

Asked by editors of *Edgewalking on the Western Rim* (Sasquatch Books, 1994)

What Was Your First Outdoor Adventure?

I got interested in the outdoors after robbing a bank.

It's true. When I was seven years old, my friend Johnny Holshauser and I robbed the local bank. This was not a joke. We were absolutely serious. We went in with our quite authentic-looking cap pistols and held the place up. It was the early 1940s and Blowing Rock, North Carolina, a small Appalachian resort community, was still mired in the Great Depression. Our strapped parents were not ungenerous, but we figured we deserved more money for candy, comic books, and other preadolescent accouterments.

In those days there was a fireworks device known as a "torpedo." Torpedoes, incongruously, were round, resembling dry, gray gumballs or jawbreakers. When you hurled one of them against a hard surface, it exploded with a loud report, like a good-size firecracker. Unbeknownst to Johnny or me, the Blowing Rock bank tellers had torpedoes on hand. When we stormed in and demanded cash, one or more tellers began surreptitiously throwing the things against the marble floors and walls.

Not surprisingly, we thought we were being fired upon. Panic-stricken, we fled, absolutely convinced there were bullets whizzing past our heads. We ran to the end of town

and high-tailed it up into the hills, where we concealed ourselves, certain the police – or maybe a posse of armed men –
would soon be after us.

In many ways, that day on the lam turned out to be one of
the finest days of our childhood. We gorged ourselves on huckleberries and teaberries (the source of the unique flavor in
Pepto-Bismol). At one point, we actually caught a fish by
splashing it out of the water onto the bank of a shallow creek.
The fish was only about four inches long, no more than a
sardine, but we built a little fire and cooked it, not bothering
with the formalities of fillet. We ate it insides and all, and we
ate it with gusto.

In the area where we were hiding, there was a fairly spectacular waterfall. Several adults had been injured while
climbing Glen Burney Falls, and rumor had it that one climber
had actually fallen to his death. That day, Johnny and I
climbed Glen Burney without a qualm. (Later, unbeknownst
to our parents and to the horror of my female cousins, we
were to scale it on numerous occasions.) Above the falls, we
discovered a ring of rhododendron bushes. In the circle's
center, the moss was as soft as nouveau-riche shag carpet.
Protected by the bushes and a rocky little grotto, it made an
ideal hideout, one which we were to make advantageous use
of over the next several years, although our life of crime was
mercifully short-lived.

Eventually, it grew dark. Owls started hooting and uniden-
tifiable things began to go bump in the night. Scared, cold, and
no longer captivated by the gastronomic charms of berries, we
lost heart and, circumventing the falls, sheepishly made our way
toward home. All afternoon, the story of our "robbery" had
been circulating in town and, to their good credit, everybody,
including the bank tellers and our families, seemed more
amused than outraged by it.

Hands uncuffed, legs unshackled, necks unnoosed, the

robbers were given dinner, baths, a stern lecture, and sent to bed.

It may or may not be true that crime doesn't pay, but our little caper had a happy ending, the best part of which was an introduction to life in the wilderness. From that day on, I spent as much time as possible in the outdoor world, finding there the kind of inner nourishment that others are said to find in the mosque, the synagogue, the church – or the bank.

Asked by *Trips*, 1989

Do You Express Your Personal Political Opinions in Your Novels?

Since liberation has always been a major theme of mine, I suppose there's an undercurrent in my novels that could be interpreted as political. On the other hand, it doesn't toe anybody's party line and it's rarely event-specific.

My approach has been to encourage readers to embrace life, on the assumption that anyone who's saying "yes" to life is automatically going to say "no" to those forces and policies that destroy life, bridle it, dull it, or render it miserable. As an advocate, I'm more akin to Zorba the Greek than to Ralph Nader.

Elliott Bay Books Newsletter, 2003

How Would You Evaluate
John Steinbeck?

Maybe what I admire most about John Steinbeck is that he never mortgaged his forty-acre heart for a suite in an ivory tower. Choosing to travel among downtrodden dreamers rather than the tuxedoed tiddly-poops of the establishment, he brought both a rawboned American romanticism and an elegant classical pathos to the stories he told about their undervalued lives. Any writer who can't be inspired by that has put his or her own heart at risk.

Asked by the Center for Steinbeck Studies, San José State University, 2002

Tell Us About Your
Favorite Car

When I drove off the used-car lot in my first Cadillac, I felt like I'd finally grown up. I mean, that car had "adult" written all over it. Unfortunately, I only kept it ninety days.

This was no adolescent rite of passage. It was 1981 and I'd been legal for so many years I could do it in my sleep. But my previous car, a hand-painted old Mercury convertible, had an air of youthful frivolity perhaps not befitting a successful author.

That Caddy, however, was solid citizen. A maroon '76 DeVille sedan, its plush interior was the color of the cranberry sauce at a Republican fund-raising dinner. Into it, I could fit my entire volleyball team, our equipment, a couple of girl-friends, and a case of beer. It was as quiet as a cathedral and so smooth it was like riding on Twinkie cream.

Problem was, it made me feel like a middle-aged Jewish dentist. Now, there's nothing wrong with middle-aged Jewish dentists: they dig impeccable root canals and make, I'm sure, fine fathers, friends, and neighbors. Well and good, but the image fit me like a mouthful of metal braces – and I had no access to laughing gas.

When my embarrassment level reached the point where I was slumping down in the seat and shielding my face while driving, I took the Cadillac into a General Motors dealership and asked to have it tricked out: wire wheels, pinstripes, landau top. Naively, I suppose, I was determined to somehow make it cool. Since I had to leave it overnight, the dealer offered to provide me with a loaner. A diabolically clever fellow, he nonchalantly sent me home in a new gold-and-black Camaro Z-28. Wow! Good golly, Miss Molly! Flying chickens in a barnyard! I'd never piloted anything remotely like it. After no more than twenty zippy miles and eight tight corners, I'd fallen hopelessly in love. The next day I zoomed back and traded in the Caddy.

I've been happily Z-ing ever since. The Camaro holds only half a volleyball team and is like riding on peanut M&M's. But it's more responsive than three June brides and a dozen bribed congressmen – and nobody asks me to cap their teeth.

Asked by *Road & Track*, June 1987

What Is Your Favorite Place
in Nature?

Back before the earth became a couch potato, content to sit around and watch the action in other galaxies, it displayed a talent for energetic geophysical innovation. Among the lesser known products of our planet's creative period is a scattering of landlocked "islands," dramatic humps of preglacial sandstone (covered nowadays with fir and madrona) rising out of the alluvial plain on which I live in northwest Washington State.

Although rugged and almost rudely abrupt, there's a feminine swell to these outcroppings that reminds me of Valkyrie breasts or, on those frequently drizzly days when they are kimonoed in mist, of scoops of Sung Dynasty puddings.

One of the larger outcroppings – called simply The Rock by its admirers – can be partially negotiated by a four-wheel-drive vehicle. I hike the last one hundred yards through tall, dark trees, and at the summit find that the hump goddesses, as usual, have rolled out the green carpet for me. There's spongy moss underfoot, a variety of grasses and ferns and more wildflowers than Heidi's goats could chew up in a fortnight.

In a few more yards, however, I find myself standing on virtually bare sandstone, and that sandstone is falling *away away away* in a plunge so steep it would be terrifying were it not so beautiful. Perched like Pan on a damp and dizzy precipice, I can look *down* on gliding eagles, into the privacy of osprey nests, across a verdant luminescence of leaf life and a hidden, lily-padded pond, where in spring a trillion frogs gossip about Kermit's residuals.

To visit The Rock is to visit a natural frontier both dangerous and comforting, hard and soft, familiar and mysterious. And like Thoreau's Walden, The Rock defines the boundary between civilization and wilderness, existing as it does twenty minutes via jeep from a bustling town, two seconds via daydream from the beginning of time.

Asked by *LIFE* magazine, 1987

Send Us a Souvenir From the Road

A few years ago, I was sitting at a battered desk in my room in the funky old wing of the Pioneer Inn, Lahaina, Maui, when I discovered the following rhapsody scratched with a ballpoint pen into the soft wooden bottom of the desk drawer.

Saxaphone
Saxiphone
Saxophone
Saxyphone
Saxephone
Saxafone

Obviously, some unknown traveler – drunk, stoned, or simply Spell-Check deprived – had been penning a postcard or letter when he or she ran headlong into Dr. Sax's marvelous instrument. I have no idea how the problem was resolved, but the confused attempt struck me as a little poem, an ode to the challenges of our written language.

I collected the "poem," and many times since, I've fantasized about how the word in question might have fit into the stranger's communiqué. For example: "When I get back from Hawaii, I'm going to blow you like a saxophone."

Or, "Not even a saxophone can help me now."

Or, "Here the saxophone (saxaphone? saxofone?) is seldom confused with the ukulele (ukalele? ukilele? ukaleli?)."

Black Book, 2002

What Is the Function of Metaphor?

If, as Terence McKenna contended, the world is actually made of language, then metaphors and similes (puns, too, I might add) extend the dimensions and expand the possibilities of the world. When both innovative and relevant, they can wake up a reader, make him or her aware, through the elasticity of verbiage, that reality – in our daily lives as well as in our stories – is less prescribed than tradition has led us to believe.

Metaphors have the capacity to heat up a scene and eternalize an image, to lift a line of prose out of the mundane mire of mere fictional reportage and lodge it in the luminous honeycomb of the collective psyche. They can squeeze meaning out of the most unlikely turnip.

On a personal level, I was asked at a bookstore reading once if my fondness for metaphors wasn't a gimmick. In response, I asked the questioner, "Were Hemingway's short declarative sentences a gimmick? Were the long convoluted sentences of Faulkner a gimmick?" In both instances, the answer is emphatically *no*. When Hemingway and Faulkner distilled their respective realities into language, what we encounter on the page is the stylistic reflection of those realities. It's how those two writers saw the world. Or, more accurately, it's how they were compelled to *represent* what they saw. In my case, because I'm fascinated by words, mythology, and transfiguration, it's hardly surprising that I'd refract life through the polychromatic lens of metaphor and simile.

Admittedly, I get a kick from simply playing with language, but I try to make it a point not to create metaphor for metaphor's sake; to never fashion them carelessly or employ them arbitrarily. I insist that whenever possible they not only spring out of trap-doors or closets but that their "Surprise!" has contextural *pertinence*.

Ultimately, I use such figures of speech to deepen the reader's subliminal understanding of the person, place, or thing that's being described. That, above everything else, validates their role as a highly effective literary device. If nothing else, they remind reader and writer alike that language is not the frosting, it's the cake.

Asked by *Inside Borders,* 2003

Are You a Realist?

According to Fellini, "The visionary is the only true realist." Before we dismiss that declaration as the ravings of a . . . well, a *visionary,* we should consider this:

Most of the activity in the universe is occurring at speeds too fast or too slow for normal human senses to register it, and most of the matter in the universe exists in amounts too vast or too tiny to be accurately observed by us. With that in mind, isn't it a bit unrealistic to talk about "realism"?

What Tom Wolfe and the other champions of naturalistic writing would have us accept as realistic content is actually the behavior patterns of a swarm of fruit flies on one bursting peach in an orchard with a thousand varieties of strange fruit stretching beyond every visible horizon. Granted, those fruit flies are pretty damn interesting, but from the standpoint of "reality" they are hardly the only game in town.

Since the so-called fabric of reality has been historically perforated with false assumptions, and is continuously stained by myriad hues of subjectivity, any of us poor fools who believe we're writing something real may actually be the unwitting butts of a fiendish cosmic joke.

On the other hand, there's a point of view shared by most mystics and many theoretical physicists that purports that everything in the universe, large or small, is simply a projection of our consciousness. So, one could make a case for *all* writers being realists, including those who write about the secret lives of inanimate objects every bit as much as those who focus on jury deliberations or coming of age in rural Nebraska.

Asked by *Contemporary Literature*, 2001

What Is the Meaning of Life?

Our purpose is to consciously, deliberately evolve toward a wiser, more liberated and luminous state of being; to return to Eden, make friends with the snake, and set up our computers among the wild apple trees.

Deep down, all of us are probably aware that some kind of mystical evolution – a melding into the godhead, into love – is our true task. Yet we suppress the notion with considerable force because to admit it is to acknowledge that most of our political gyrations, religious dogmas, social ambitions, and financial ploys are not merely counterproductive but trivial. Our mission is to jettison those pointless preoccupations and take on once again the primordial cargo of inexhaustible ecstasy. Or, barring that, to turn out a good thin-crust pizza and a strong glass of beer.

Asked by *LIFE* magazine, 1991

Tom Robbins titles can be obtained from

NO EXIT PRESS